A Gl

Lynne & Jim —

Thank you so much for your
kindness and friendship in opening
up your home. We look forward to
seeing you all again on another
swing through Seattle — or better yet,
come to Malaysia ☺

Peace —
Dave & Julie

A GREAT WORK

A Conversation with Nehemiah for People
(Who Want To Be) Doing Great Works

Jon Swanson

When word came to Sanballat,
Tobiah, Geshem the Arab and the rest of
our enemies that I had rebuilt the wall and not
a gap was left in it—though up to that time I
had not set the doors in the gates— Sanballat
and Geshem sent me this message: "Come, let
us meet together in one of the villages on the
plain of Ono."

But they were scheming to harm me; so I
sent messengers to them with this reply: "I am
carrying on a great project and cannot go
down. Why should the work stop while I leave
it and go down to you?" Four times they sent
me the same message, and each time I gave
them the same answer.

Nehemiah 6:2-4

CONTENTS

FOREWORD

HOPE SWANSON

With the rise of self-publishing, books that have no business being sold are regularly finding their way onto Amazon.

Someone has a cool life story or wrote a great creative writing sample for a class, and suddenly people are saying "You should write a book." They don't really mean it and would never purchase the finished product, but it's what the writer wants to hear. He or she decides to sit down and type up a manuscript. Because self-publishing doesn't require anyone's approval, the writer can put it up for sale and then sink into a depression when it doesn't sell more than the few pity copies bought by relatives and close friends.

So why are we publishing this? Why is this book more worthy of publication than any of the others?

Unbiased opinion: my dad is a great writer. Seriously, if I didn't think he was talented, I wouldn't be spending time doing this. He writes well, he writes good, he writes to teach, and people learn. He has made friends all over the country and world over the past several years as he has written posts on various blogs, spoken at conferences, and tweeted about the coffee being ready. (You don't have to take my word for it. Check out 300wordsaday.com or follow him on Twitter at @jnswanson to find out for yourself.) And the fact that he spent over a decade studying and teaching communication and rhetoric, and a lifetime working on understanding what it means to follow Christ gives him some credibility. (Not to mention that he's already published three ebooks that have sold pretty well.) It's quality, thoughtful, insightful writing. He did the necessary research. He worked to understand, and it's worth sharing with those who struggle with the Old Testament.

People don't read the Old Testament. Okay, so we read Psalms and Proverbs, parts of Isaiah, parts of the Pentateuch, and other stories that we think are cool (Esther, Ruth, the anointing of David, etc.). But Nehemiah? "Oh, he's the one who built the wall, right? Yeah, I kinda remember reading that story in my Read-the-whole-Bible-in-a-Year plan. I guess it was pretty cool." Dad's book takes us into the story. The subtitle is "A Conversation with Nehemiah for People (who want to be) Doing Great Works." Sometimes Dad might sound a little crazy because he's saying that he's having conversations with Nehemiah, but that's what it's like. You'll get over it. It's a different way of reading the OT. As I read Dad's book I am constantly reminded that Nehemiah was a real guy who actually oversaw the rebuilding of the wall around Jerusalem, who actually faced opposition, who actually prayed and fasted for four months until the king asked him what was up. Readers will have an understanding of Nehemiah that you just can't get from reading a traditional commentary. Unless you actually understand traditional commentaries, in which case I commend you. But read this book. It's worth your time.

It's quality. It's different. It's helpful.

It's worthy of publication.

-Hope Swanson

PREFACE

Conversations with Nehemiah

You want to do something great.

We all want to do great things. We all want to change the world. We all want to do something that matters, to be someone who matters. I do. You do, too.

We don't have to be in charge, we tell ourselves. In fact, we're not sure we could be. But we're tired of just doing stuff for someone else's agenda.

You and I have both read too many management books, leadership books, greatness books. They are full of great ideas, promises, guidelines. But maybe we need to look at the Bible. After all, people who hang around church have heard that the Bible is a place to look for significance. But we don't know where to start.

I'd like to suggest the story of Nehemiah.

Nehemiah is a book in the Old Testament, between Ezra and Esther. It used to be packaged with Ezra. In most top-selling Bibles, it's not any more. It hasn't been for many centuries. And Nehemiah is the lead character in that book.

Nehemiah seems like a textbook. I think it is. I think God knows exactly the story he wanted to tell about a life depending on him and doing a great work. So when we read it, it should come as no surprise that it makes sense.

I've read *Nehemiah* several times during the past four decades. During the summer of 2012, I started reading it differently. I taught it with a couple of small groups. I wrote at 300wordsaday.com about the study I was doing. I decided to write a weekly newsletter about what I was learning. And as I was writing the first issue, I discovered I was having a conversation with Nehemiah.

No, really.

And this is a collection of those conversations, occurring over coffee and tea. I know, of course, that coffee was identified as a drink a thousand years or so after Nehemiah lived. But for a guy who shows up in 445 BC, he seems to enjoy it. And some of our conversations are filling in things not covered in the book of *Nehemiah* and the rest of the Old Testament. But I have worked to maintain the integrity of the Biblical story.

PROLOGUE

God and Israel: The Real Story of True Love, Rescue, Adultery, Exile, and Restoration

"A Great Work" could be the season title for the television epic, "God and Israel: The Real Story of True Love, Rescue, Adultery, Exile, and Restoration." Set in 445 BC, this particular season introduces a new character, a civil servant named Nehemiah. It is possible to start watching the series with this season. We do it all the time. But just as a well-created series rewards those who watch more than one season, reading Nehemiah will be richer with a recap of the highlights of previous seasons. To understand "A Great Work", we need to go back a millennium and more.

Let's start near the end of one of the early seasons, set sometime between 1500 and 1200 BC. "Exodus" features Moses. He was a leader with a broken spirit. Forty years of elite Egyptian leadership training, then forty years attempting to lead sheep. The early episodes leave us wondering how he will recover. But in the episode, "Burning Bush," Moses gets a life work: "Go rescue your people." He does. They are rescued, and after forty years in the wilderness, Moses leads the nation to the edge of the end of their journey. Before he dies, before they take on their next battles, Moses spends a special two-hour episode called "Deuteronomy" giving his last lecture. Full of flashbacks and huge crowd shots, this episode reviews the whole history of Moses and God and Israel.

At the end, Moses is blunt: "You are going to screw up." But then he left the people with this promise:

> *When all these blessings and curses I have set before you come on you and you take them to heart wherever the Lord your God disperses you among the nations, and when you and your children return to the Lord your God and obey him with all your heart and with all your soul according to everything I command you today, then the Lord your God will restore your fortunes and have compassion on you and gather you again from all the nations where he scattered you. Even if you have been banished to the most distant land under the heavens, from there the Lord your God will gather you and bring you back. He will bring you to the land that belonged to your ancestors, and you will take possession of it. He will make you more prosperous and numerous than your ancestors.*[1]

The "Exodus" season ends with Moses dying on a mountain overlooking the promised land, then dissolves to a glimpse of Joshua, his military aide, standing up looking across the Jordan at that same land. In this Prologue, we aren't going to

---

1. *Deuteronomy 30:1-5.*

look at any of the next seasons, though they have intriguing lead characters. Caleb, poster child for the IARP (Israelite Association of Retired Persons), leading his clan into battle at age 120. Saul, David, and Solomon, the only kings of Israel who ever led all twelve tribes. And the seasons are compelling. "Everyone Knows Best: the End of *Judges*", "Head and Shoulders: the First King", "Hairy and Baldy, the True Story of Elijah and Elisha".

But we are moving past all those stories. We fast-forward several centuries, from the end of "Exodus" to the last season of "Chronicles of the Kings". As we move, we see the people of Israel transformed from immigrants to conquering nation to civil war to decline.

And then it happens. The diaspora Moses warned about actually happens. Running from 604 BC to 587 BC, "Jerusalem's End" is a brutal season. Every episode ends with a cliffhanger, and in the next episode people have fallen off the cliff.[2] By the end of the season, all that is left of Jerusalem is ruins, piles of burnt rubble, and a few shepherds.

We get to "Exile, Part One." This season features Daniel. Most people only watch a couple episodes from this season. "Fiery Furnace" tells the story of three of Daniel's friends. "Lion's Den", from near the end of the season, has Daniel risking his life for what he believed. There are several pecu-

2. Jeremiah, for example, talks about people playing Egypt against Babylon. And 2 Chronicles 36 describes a series of kings. Each one serves for a bit and then is hauled away to Babylon by Nebuchadnezzar. Finally, the city of Jerusalem is destroyed.

liar dream sequences in this season as well. But a major theme of the season is Daniel's significant role in government.

The season starts in 604 BC, with Daniel and many other bright young men being hauled away from Jerusalem in chains. It is the first of several waves of roundups by the Babylonian armies. By taking the next generation of leadership, two things happen: Jerusalem loses a generation, and Babylon gains talent. And Daniel is talented. He is a skilled administrator, trusted by the king, survives attacks on his religious beliefs, and serves two different empires (Babylon and Persia).

To understand Daniel's work, we need to look at one of the more challenging dramatic elements of the "God and Israel" series. There are several seemingly random episodes where the author steps in front of the camera and speaks. These "voice of God" episodes have different characters, but all of these episodes, which are found in many seasons, are titled "Prophet". The episode most helpful in understanding Daniel is "Prophet: Jeremiah's Letter." During the early episodes of "Exile, Part One", a letter appears, carried from Jerusalem to the people, like Daniel, living in Babylon. After assuring the people that everything is going the way God warned them, the letter says "seek the peace and prosperity of the city to which I have carried you into exile. Pray to the Lord for it, because if it prospers, you too will prosper."[3] And, Jeremiah says, the exile will last for seventy years.

The letter arrived while Daniel was a young man training for bureaucratic service. We don't know whether he read it when it arrived. It is clear, however, that he worked hard for the peace and prosperity of the city. We know Daniel does eventually read the letter, about sixty years after it arrived. By then, the Babylonian empire had been conquered by the Persians, and Daniel is serving the new government.

Cyrus, the ruler, had been predicted by a Jewish prophet to allow the exile to end. When Daniel realizes that he may be within a few years of the end of the exile, he prays. And in his prayer, he refers to the warnings Moses made. He acknowledges the sin that brought about the exile. And he begs God for action.

Now, our God, hear the prayers and petitions of your servant. For your sake, Lord, look with favor on your desolate sanctuary. Give ear, our God, and hear; open your eyes and see the desolation of the city that bears your Name. We do not make requests of you because we are righteous, but because of your great mercy. Lord, listen! Lord, forgive! Lord, hear and act! For your sake, my God, do not delay, because your city and your people bear your Name.[4]

3. Jeremiah 29:7. The letter was written around 597, after the first wave of captives were taken, before the final burning of Jerusalem.
4. *Daniel 9:17-19.*

Soon, there is action. In 538, Cyrus the Persian gives the Jews permission to return to Jerusalem. During the next 100 years, some Jews go back. The temple is slowly rebuilt. But no one can accomplish any significant work rebuilding the walls. In fact, at one point the king orders an end to attempts to rebuild. Nearly 170 years after the beginning of the exile, one hundred years after Cyrus ended the exile, Jerusalem is still a ruined city.

But then we see the previews for the new season. A man called Nehemiah is working for King Artexerxes of Persia. He had a civil service job, working in the palace. He was a sommelier, a wine steward, one of the cupbearers to the king. He carried the cup to the king, tested it for poison, and then served it. As a result, he was also a trusted member of the King's court.

Day after day, Nehemiah does his work. And the season starts.

It's evening. There's a knock on the door.

1

DOING SOMETHING
THAT MATTERS

Nehemiah 1

Thanks for asking me to tell you about Nehemiah.

This isn't where I was going to start. I had a great essay prepared about Nehemiah's planning process. I wanted to talk about his leadership. But something wasn't quite right about it. So I was sitting in my office talking with Nehemiah.

I've been doing that a lot lately. I read and think and try to understand what he was doing. It's a result of how I teach when I teach from the Bible. I want to see "Bible people" as real people in real contexts. Even if they actually were living about 445 BC.

And in the process of thinking, I started talking to Nehemiah. I asked, "Why did you go so over the top emotionally when you heard from your brother Hanani?"

Because Nehemiah had. Gone over the top that is. His brother came from Jerusalem to Susa, about 900 miles, about the distance from Fort Wayne, Indiana to Alva, Oklahoma (or Dallas to Chicago). When his brother told Nehemiah that Jerusalem was in ruins and the gates were burned, Nehemiah sat down and wept. Then he spent days mourning and fasting and praying.

"Jerusalem," Nehemiah said to me. "He was talking about *Jerusalem*."

"I know," I said, "But weeping and fasting and praying and looking awful? The walls had been down for nearly a century and a half. This was not new news."

He put down his coffee cup. Neither of us is used to him drinking coffee. Seeing this courtly leader holding a chipped coffee mug instead of a gold wine goblet is odd. And he doesn't know you hold a mug to think.

"You need to understand how I grew up," he said. "You know how you heard stories from your mom about how your great-grandfather left Sweden and left his wife and son for a decade while he went to Wisconsin to make a new life? You remember how she wanted you to have a sense of the sacrifice?"

I nodded.

"When I was three or four, sometimes in the evening my mother looked west. I thought she was looking at the sunset until one night I heard her humming. I listened. I heard her start singing:

By the rivers of Babylon we sat and wept
when we remembered Zion.
There on the poplars we hung our harps,

for there our captors asked us for songs,
our tormentors demanded songs of joy;
they said, "Sing us one of the songs of Zion!"
How can we sing the songs of the Lord
while in a foreign land?"[1]

"It was so melancholy. As a little one I couldn't handle the pain in her voice. I walked away.

"When I got older, she started to teach it to me. It's what you call Psalm 137. And I understood why she waited. The end of it talks about Edom and Babylon. In one of those sections you never read, the song talks about tossing infants...never mind.

"And of course, this wasn't about her own life, exactly. She had learned the song from her father who learned it from his father. But it was his father who had lived it. Who had watched the siege of Jerusalem. Who had watched the temple burn. Who had seen the infants killed."

He stopped. I waited. I had not expected this. *Nehemiah* was a book to me. Something I would read five chapters of in a day while reading through the Bible in a year. But sitting across from me was a real person. With a history. With a story.

"Growing up, many of us sang the songs of exile. We listened to the stories of the prophets who warned the people of the danger of ignoring God, of becoming gods themselves. We knew the exile was a result of not paying atten-

---

1. *Psalm 137:1-4*

tion to the warnings. And we learned the pilgrimage songs, the songs of ascent.[2] Songs about the annual journeys to Jerusalem, to the city of David and the city of God. To the Temple. Even though no one knew exactly when we'd need them again, we learned them.

"And then the exile was over. We could go back.

"The first groups were hopeful. They were going to the homeland no one knew. A generation went. Work started on rebuilding. And then there was another wave. We had watched the Persians conquer the Babylonians. There were stories about starting and stopping, stories about the temple.

"Eventually, my brother went to Judah. I had a good job in the palace, but I was so proud of my little brother, so thrilled to have a connection. And we waited to hear about the great work, the restoration of the city.

"One day my brother showed up unexpectedly. But that's how everyone showed up back then. Unannounced. I was so excited to hear the news of the rebuilding, of the homeland. Lots of my people were comfortable in Babylon, but those of us who cared about returning to our homeland were hopeful.

"And when I heard from Hanani that nothing had changed, I was devastated. The breath went out of me. Do you know what it is like to spend your whole life and your parents' whole lives and your grandparents' whole lives

---

2. Psalms 120-134 are subtitled "Song of Ascent". Eugene Peterson talks about them as pilgrimage songs in *A Long Obedience in the Same Direction*, a book that changed my life years ago (Downers Grove, IL: InterVarsity Press, 1980).

retelling stories of what went wrong and what would be made right, lamenting the downfall, praying for the return? And then to hear that the people who went back, who could do something, were in despair? That after two generations and more, the walls were still in ruins, the gates still gaping and charred?

"It was more than I could handle. The city was in ruins. Someone needed to decide to rebuild. And somehow, unlikely as it was, I knew it might be me. I knew that I was going to have to give my one and only life to do something. To make a change. To take everything that I knew and throw it into this."

Nehemiah slowly slipped back into his chair. I realized that he had fallen on his knees while he was talking.

I sat still. I thought of my own life, of the stories I learned about things that matter.

He smiled. "I get carried away. Sorry."

He leaned back in the chair and looked around my office. At the books. At the coffee mugs. At the pictures of family.

"You know, sometimes I wonder," he said. "If I knew that it would take the rest of my life, that I would spend a decade and more at the edges of the empire, would I have started this work? If I had known that I would fear and work and argue and defend. That I would give up all that was here in Susa for all that wasn't there in Jerusalem. That I would work all that time and still wonder whether anyone's life was really different, would I have done it again?"

His eyes stopped wandering. He leaned forward and looked at me. He said, "If you had something that mattered that much, wouldn't you start working on it, no matter what?"

I closed my eyes and leaned back in the chair. I was too emotional to answer. When I looked up, he was gone. But his question is still in my heart.

"If you had something that mattered that much, wouldn't you start working on it, no matter what?"

2

A LONG TIME PRAYING

Nehemiah 1

People ask me to pray *about* things all the time. And I have written a lot about prayer. But I don't very often listen to someone praying and then say "How did you do that?" It feels strange.

The last time Nehemiah and I were talking, I realized that he was the perfect person to ask. Prayer often shows up in the book of *Nehemiah*, from the middle of the first chapter to the very last sentence.

I looked at him. "So, your brother comes, you pray, ask God for favor, and the next day at work, the King asks you what's wrong. That's amazing!"

He coughed discretely. "You did say that you read my book, didn't you? Do you have a copy here somewhere?" He looked around.

I turned the screen toward him, browser open to an

online Bible. He ignored it. It was pretty clear that he wanted *me* to read.

"Oh, right. It says that you wept and mourned *for days*. I bet you were pretty hungry after that week. How do you pray that long?"

He coughed again. The polite habits of a wine steward last for millennia I guess. "Do you have a calendar?" he asked. I pointed to the one on the wall.

"That's yours. Where's mine?"

I looked at him.

"I don't want to point out the obvious," he said, "but the book is pretty clear about my brother coming in Chislev and the King talking to me in Nisan. You probably should look at a calendar with months rather than days, and one with my months rather than yours."

I looked it up. Four months. That's how long from Chislev to Nisan. The period of prayer Nehemiah describes is like starting a period of fasting and mourning and praying in late October and staying with it until the end of February.

I asked him how it was possible to pray the same thing for four months. And how he could not eat for all that time.

"I know, right? I'm working in the palace, great meals. Even after Daniel's healthy eating experiment, there was plenty of food we could eat.[1] But I knew that fasting was something done in times of serious approach to God. And I was serious.

---

1. Nehemiah was talking about a vegetable and water eating plan Daniel used at the beginning of the exile that Nehemiah came at the end of. You can read about it in Daniel 1.

14

"In my grief, I started looking at the prophets, the people who had written about the exile. And I found words from Isaiah that gave me hope, words from a hundred years before me. Isaiah wrote, 'Your people will rebuild the ancient ruins and will raise up the age-old foundations. You will be called Repairer of Broken Walls, Restorer of Streets with Dwellings.'[2]

"That was exactly what I wanted to do. But what would it take? I read the context of the prophecy, what comes immediately before the promise.

"Isaiah talked about the kind of fasting that God wanted.[3] It's fasting that shares meals with people who need the food rather than just not eating. It's a life of justice, of being a leader who cares for people, of looking for underdogs and helping them. It's a life of spending yourself on behalf of the hungry.

"It changed everything I thought about how to pray and how to follow God and how to lead. I spent four months letting that work into my life.

- Every day I said, 'God you are the faithful one, the committed one. Please listen to me.'
- Every day I said, 'We have sinned. Generations of us, yes, but my family too. And I have sinned, God.' That reminder was important to me as I was learning about sharing and justice and compassion. I learned to look at my own behavior.
- Every day I reminded God about the stories of

2. Isaiah 58:12.
3. Isaiah 58:5-14.

repentance from Moses and from Isaiah. And when I did that, I was reminding myself.[4]

- And every day I wanted to be ready for serving the King."

I held up my hand. "When you say "King", do you mean your king, Artexerxes, or your King, God?"

"Yes."

I thought about Nehemiah's words. Four months, every day, morning and evening. Four months learning to give up deserved meals to share with others. Four months of learning to discern misappropriated power. Four months of developing integrity of heart and mind. Four months of going to work while still going to God. Four months of asking God to give him favor in the King's eyes.

"Are you saying," I asked, "That every morning and every evening, your prayer was simply acknowledging sin, asking God to listen to you, and asking for a good reputation with your boss?"

He nodded. "It's simple to say. It's harder to do than you would think."

Finally, I looked at him and said, "You spent more time fasting and praying than you did rebuilding the walls. So which part was the great work?"

"Precisely," he replied. With a nod, he walked out.

I looked at Nehemiah's prayer.[5] Morning and evening,

---

4. There is more about this heritage of prayer in the next chapter.
5. Nehemiah 1:5-12.

I've been looking at it. And at my heart. And thinking that four months may not be long enough.

3

PRAYING IN A HERITAGE OF PRAYER

Nehemiah 1

One day, I got curious about Nehemiah's prayer. I searched an online Bible for the phrase: "great and awesome God." It's a phrase Nehemiah uses at the beginning of his confessional prayer, the prayer he prays for months. I discovered that he wasn't original. The phrase had been used before.

"Why were you looking at my words?" he asked. He had been sitting in his chair in the corner of my office while I was searching.

I thought about it. "I'm not sure. Something about the phrase sounded familiar. For awhile I thought it was like 'the great and powerful Oz'. But that wasn't it. When I went looking, I found that Daniel started a prayer almost the same way. Did you know about his prayer when you were pray-ing?"

"The prayer in what you call Daniel 9?" Nehemiah asked. He looked out the window. "It would have been so much easier for us to have chapter and verse numbers.[1] We just memorized everything."

"But did you memorize *Daniel's* prayer?" I was persistent.

Nehemiah just looked at me.

"Here's why I'm asking. Your prayer sounds very much like Daniel's prayer. You are both calling out to 'the great and awesome God.' You both describe him as the God 'who keeps his covenant of love with those who love him and keep his commandments.'[2] The exact same words. I want to know if everyone talked to God that way. I want to know if that phrasing should be a formula for us. I want to know whether you and Daniel were part of a Jewish civil service prayer and Bible study group."

Nehemiah smiled slightly. "Why do you ask that, in par-ticular?"

For once I felt like a teacher when talking with Nehemiah. Or a forensic Bible student. "I realized that both you and Daniel were in positions of significant trust with foreign kings. Your book starts about 100 years after Daniel's finishes, but we don't know how many years passed

---

1. Though we think of the chapters and verses and headers as part of "the Bible", they are not part of the original writings. Verses and chapters were added for convenience in study, but they can interfere in tracking a thought. And the headings? Those are added by editors of various versions. They are the most basic version of commentary on the text. But they are not the text.

2. Daniel 9:4 and Nehemiah 1:5.

between you. And then the appearance of Mordecai in a position of responsibility in the court of your king's predecessor suggests that there were people a baton pass apart who served the king and followed God.[3] Is it a spiritual support group for those who would otherwise feel alone in leadership?"

"I'm not going to say more than the story says," Nehemiah replied eventually. "But Jeremiah told us very early in the exile to

> seek the peace and prosperity of the city to which I have carried you into exile. Pray to the Lord for it, because if it prospers, you too will prosper.[4]

"Daniel, Mordecai, and I took that instruction seriously. Serving the king well *was* obeying God. The same phrasing doesn't have to mean that we were connected in the way that you suggest. However, it is a good model for praying which I probably heard from others, just as you pick up phrases that are helpful. I will give you this, just as I wasn't the only one praying for Jerusalem in my time, Daniel wasn't alone in his time." Nehemiah smiled at me. "But you are missing much in Daniel's prayer, and mine, if you stop with the wording of the first sentence. Look at the whole prayer."

I looked. "You both talk to God about disobedience.

---

3. Mordecai was a relative of Esther, mentioned in the book by that name. At the beginning of *Esther*, Mordecai is serving in the court of King Ahasuarus (Xerxes). By the end of *Esther*, he has a senior leadership position.

4. *Jeremiah* 29:7.

You both include yourselves by saying 'we' but you point to your ancestors."

"That's a good start." Nehemiah said. "When talking to God about wrongdoing, it's wise to not focus just on what 'they' have done. That feels like blaming. Both Daniel and I owned up to being part of the community that had sinned. What else do you see?"

I hesitated. "It seems like Daniel is focusing more on the people who did wrong. You are focusing more on wanting God to keep a promise."

"Very good. That's what happens when two people look at the same warnings and promises from two different places."

I must have looked confused.

"You see how Daniel and I both refer to Moses in our prayer? We were both looking at what Moses said centuries before. We were both aware of what Solomon had prayed at the dedication of the temple.

"Both Moses and Solomon warned about what would happen when our people turned from God and both told us what God would do if we returned. When we turned, we would be scattered. Moses didn't say 'if', he said 'when'. Four hundred years apart, our people heard those warnings. And then God waited another four hundred years before allowing Jerusalem to be destroyed. Generation after generation, king after king, prophet after prophet. You can read for yourself that there were many, many opportunities. But eventually, God showed us that he was willing to have the city of God destroyed to show that he cared more about his people than his city."

I held up my hand. "Can you wait a bit while I read those stories?" Nehemiah nodded and walked out. I heard him in the kitchen fixing coffee. I read the words of Moses in Deuteronomy.

> All the nations will ask: "Why has the Lord done this to this land? Why this fierce, burning anger?" And the answer will be: "It is because this people abandoned the covenant of the Lord, the God of their ancestors, the covenant he made with them when he brought them out of Egypt. They went off and worshiped other gods and bowed down to them, gods they did not know, gods he had not given them.[5]

I read the words of Solomon in 1 Kings:

> and if they turn back to you with all their heart and soul in the land of their enemies who took them captive, and pray to you toward the land you gave their ancestors, toward the city you have chosen and the temple I have built for your Name; then from heaven, your dwelling place, hear their prayer and their plea, and uphold their cause.[6]

The warnings were clear. The promise was great. I was ready to talk again. And Nehemiah walked back in, carrying two mugs.

5. *Deuteronomy 29:22-30:5.*
6. *1 Kings 8:46-53.*

Nehemiah spoke first. "Daniel looked at those warnings and promises from Moses and Solomon. He read Jeremiah's comment about a seventy-year exile and looked at the calendar. He did the math from his own trip into exile in 604 and realized that the seventy years could be completed in four or five years. He wanted to be sure that our people could go home as soon as possible. So Daniel was intent on letting God know that he, Daniel, knew how serious the sin had been. It was a very powerful time of confession. You know that feeling."

I nodded.

"It's important to understand, too, that Daniel had watched the sins of the kings and princes and ancestors. Daniel had been in Jerusalem; he had seen how awful the disobedience was. Daniel was praying as an old man who had spent a lifetime understanding the consequences of sinning against God."

I nodded. "I love Daniel's closing: 'We do not make requests of you because we are righteous, but because of your great mercy.'"[7]

Nehemiah smiled. "And that's what gave me such hope one hundred years later. God's mercy had ended the exile. God's mercy had allowed people to rebuild the temple."

I interrupted. "But there was still the promise that Moses made, the other half of his message."

"Exactly," Nehemiah said. "That's *my* focus. Moses said that if we turned back to God, he would bring us back from

7. Daniel 9:18.

the distant nations. What could be more distant than Susa? So I was reminding God that I was praying and we were praying and it was time to go home."

I leaned forward. "That's what you meant by looking at the same story from two places. Moses and Solomon looked at the future and gave warnings and promises. Jeremiah wrote from the middle of the story and reminded the people that God was working out a plan. Daniel looked at the warnings and was convicted. You looked at the promises and were hopeful."

Nehemiah nodded. "But all of us were looking at God. His words were the same for all of us. Our situations highlighted them differently and gave them greater dimension."

He set his mug down. "So are you still worried about whether the words of my prayer were original? Or is it enough that I was faithful to a long thread of consistent conversation with God?"

I looked down. "Faithful is good."

I looked up. He was gone.

So I tried it myself.

Lord, the God of heaven, the great and awesome God, who keeps his covenant of love with those who love him and keep his commandments, let your ear be attentive and your eyes open to hear the prayer your servant is praying before you day and night for your servants, the people of Israel.[8]

"And me," I said. "Please listen to me."

8. *Nehemiah 1:5-6.*

25

PREPARING FOR THE WORK

Nehemiah 2

Having conversations with Nehemiah is risky. I had just finished writing about daily prayer. I went up to take a shower. And as I was turning the water on I said, out loud, "Wait a minute. Is that all you did for four months?"

I'm pretty sure Nancy didn't hear me.

But Nehemiah did. He was waiting for me when I went back down to my office.

"Of course not," he said, answering my question. "I prayed. I went to work. I started paying attention to the needs around me. I talked more with my brother, who also started praying. And the strangest thing started to happen. One day I was thinking about the situation and thought, 'The city is in ruins and the gates are burned.' Just that simple. In the middle of preparing the king's wine, I would start thinking 'You know, if I did go to Jerusalem, we'd need to get some lumber to rebuild those gates.' Listening to reports come in from the provinces, I'd think, 'We would need to get permission to pass through their territory.'

"After four months of talking to God and thinking about the problem, I had a whole plan worked out. I wrote it on the papyrus on my table. I called it *What I would do if God gave me a chance.*'"

I leaned forward, "So that day when the king asked what was wrong, you were ready?"

"Absolutely. I mean, I was terrified about getting caught looking sad in front of the king. I was surprised that this was the day, but I realized that God was ready."

I said, "But I always thought God just gave you the plan instantly when you were in the situation. Like Jesus said would happen when the disciples were brought before judges.[1] I didn't know you actually thought about all this."

Nehemiah sat up straight. "Oh, I don't have any question about God being able to work that way. But I had four months to think and pray and research. If I hadn't used that time, I would have been pretty irresponsible."

I couldn't tell if he was hurt or not.

After we talked, I decided that it was time to share an essay I wrote about Nehemiah's plan. I call it, "Nehemiah's five-step plan to rebuild a destroyed city by asking a foreign king to give you all the supplies you need." Or that's what I wanted to call it. Nehemiah said that was too long. So now

---

1. In Mark 13:11, we Jesus tells the disciples that they will be arrested, but they are not to worry beforehand what to say. Instead, they are to trust the Holy Spirit. But that doesn't seem to be an excuse for never planning.

I call it, "Five steps to God-shaped plans." Nehemiah still calls it "my life."

***

"The city is in ruins and the gates are burned."

Nehemiah lived in Susa, a city in Persia, in modern Iran. Nehemiah's brother came 900 miles from Jerusalem to visit. When Nehemiah asked how things were back in their home country, his brother said *that Jerusalem was in ruins and the gates were burned.*[2] When Nehemiah's boss, King Artaxerxes, asked him why he was so sad, Nehemiah said that *the city of his ancestors was ruined and the gates were burned.*[3] When Nehemiah got to Jerusalem to begin his work, he did a late-night tour to see that *the walls were ruined and the gates were burned.*[4] When Nehemiah finally talked to the leaders in Jerusalem about the work in front of them, he said "*the city is ruined and the gates are burned.*"[5]

Four times in the first two chapters. Every time Nehemiah has to explain the problem, it's very simple: **the city is ruined and the gates are burned.**

So what's the point? It's the first point of Nehemiah's great work.

1. **Nehemiah had a clear picture of what was wrong.**
He was able to summarize the problem for himself, and for others, in vivid, factual, brief words.

---

2. Nehemiah 1:3.
3. Nehemiah 2:3.
4. Nehemiah 2:13.
5. Nehemiah 2:17.

Let's take a look at the other four parts of Nehemiah's plan.

2. A simple confidence that God was involved from the start.

This may be the hardest truth for many of us. We don't know whether God is talking to us. We aren't sure whether an idea is from God or from our own imagination or from somewhere else. We don't understand how God gives ideas

So let's look at the story from the first two chapters of Nehemiah's memoir:

- Nehemiah's brother brings him news.
- Nehemiah spends time praying, fasting, mourning.
- Nehemiah talks to God and ends that prayer with this request: "Give me favor with that man."
- And then, Nehemiah goes to work; the King asks him what he wants to do, and we read, "I prayed and said to the king..."

I think that Nehemiah had a pretty clear picture of what he would say if the king ever asked. He had spent four months thinking and praying. And I think this reflects his belief that God actually answers prayer. Nehemiah assumed that *if* he was asking God for wisdom and opportunity, then the ideas that came, the plans that were laid out *were* the wisdom. When the king asked the question, that was the opportunity Nehemiah had *asked* for.

3. A simple proposal of what to do.

When the king asked Nehemiah what he wanted, Nehemiah said, "Send me to rebuild the walls." When

Nehemiah told the people what they were going to do, he said "Rebuild the walls."

Yes, in every project there are details. There are strategies. There are all kinds of plans that need to be laid out. But Nehemiah had distilled everything into a simple statement: *"The city is in ruins. The gates are burned. Let's rebuild the walls."*

4. A specific plan of how to proceed.

Okay, now life gets more complicated. The planning phase can overwhelm the project. But Nehemiah has worked out the details. So when the king asks questions, Nehemiah has clear answers.

- I will need a leave of absence from work, so here's how long I need.
- We will need permission as we travel, so give me letters.
- We will need wood to rebuild the gates, so give me a letter to the forester.

And he knew what he needed to do when he got to Jerusalem.

- Rest without telling people the plan.
- See for himself how badly the city was damaged.
- Gather the leadership and tell them the plan.

The specificity of Nehemiah's plan is remarkable. And the steps of the plan are a pretty good model for anyone needing to know how to approach a challenging project.

5. A commitment to act on the plan.

No matter how good a plan, it is useless unless you actually do stuff. Nehemiah actually did stuff. When the king asked, he answered. When the king approved the plan, Nehemiah left. He did every step in his plan with confidence. And when he faced opposition, he was able to tell his distractors, "Here's what we're doing. You can't stop us."

So what?

I don't know what your great work is. For some of my friends, it starts with one of these:

- "Kids the age of my daughter are being bought and sold."
- "I don't know enough about the Bible to answer my friend's questions."
- "Families are broken and the kids are getting lost."
- "There are people in that village who don't have a Bible in their heart language."
- "We've abandoned the people around our church."

Whether you are leading an organization or leading yourself, I commend Nehemiah's five steps to you.

***

"That was pretty good," Nehemiah said. "That's what I did. But I wasn't following any points like that. I was just doing what made sense."

"I know," I replied. "But some of us haven't learned that sense. Until we watch you, that is."

5

LEADING THE PEOPLE WHO ARE ALREADY THERE

Nehemiah 3

"Help," I whispered.

Nehemiah was sitting in my office. Just sitting. In my mind, I was running through a long list of projects in front of me. I was feeling a huge backlog.

Finally, I turned my chair and looked at him.

"Help," I said again.

"What makes you think I can help you?" he replied. He lifted his coffee mug and sipped, looking right at me the whole time.

"You had a huge project. You got it done fast. And you weren't any more prepared to lead than I am."

He stiffened.

I started babbling. "I mean, you had a great job and a

great reputation with the king, but you weren't in the first chair. You weren't a king, you weren't a general, you weren't a manager."

He set his mug down very deliberately. "I think we need to talk about my preparation sometime soon," he said. "But that won't help you right now. You are feeling swamped. And you need some insight for the middle of the project."

"Exactly," I said.

"Okay. Read chapter 3 of my memoir. It's the list of names."

"I'd rather not," I said. I had looked at that list while trying to read through the book. It was one of several lists, all of which I skimmed.

He looked at me and said quietly, "Do you want my help or not?"

I stopped. "Okay. I'll read it. But give me a summary."

He leaned back in the chair, a teacher ready to talk for a while. "I'll give you five lessons that will help you lead in your great work. But they will only make sense if you read."

I nodded.

He held up a finger. "**Lesson number one: If you read closely, chapter three is a circle–not a list.**"

He knew he'd lost me already. This didn't sound like a leadership lesson or a practical principle.

"It's not," he said, reading my thoughts. "The only way you can learn *from* the book is to learn to *how to read* the book. You have always read this chapter like a book chapter, and it looked like a list of names. If you look closely, this isn't a line, it's a circle. This is a panorama shot. It starts at the Sheep Gate and ends at the Sheep Gate. Instead of sitting and reading this, stand up and point to the parts of the circle that represent who is building where."

I waited.

"No, really, stand up. Read the names, look around the circle."

So I did. And he was right.

"Wait a minute," I said. "When I read it that way, it looks like the goldsmiths and merchants are on either side of the Sheep Gate. And so are the priests."[1]

"Exactly," he said. "That's where the temple was. That's where the trade happened. If you keep looking at the lists, you might see more patterns. But let's move on.

"Lesson two: Most of the people rebuilding the wall didn't come with me. They were on location and had been for years."

"How does that help *me* in the middle of my project list?" I was feeling a little selfish. After all, I have the deadlines. Nehemiah is dead.

Nehemiah answered, "What if all around you are people who are anxious to work on parts of the project of rebuilding the same wall you are interested in? What if they've just felt stuck? They are already here. They just need help."

"But that's the problem," I said. "*I* need help. They might need help, but I'm who matters at the moment."

Nehemiah looked at me. "What kind of help do you need?"

---

1. Nehemiah 3:1; 3:32.

"The city is ruined and the gates are burned."

He smiled, "That was my problem. What's yours?"

It took me a little while, but I figured out a list of three or four of the biggest projects facing me right now. I told him the highlights.

"What kind of help can *you* give?" he asked.

I just stared at him. "What do you mean?"

He was patient, "What do you know how to do, whether it applies to this project or not?"

"According to the 'StrengthsFinder', my strengths are strategic, ideation, empathy, intellection, and connectedness."[2]

"Does everyone have those strengths? Do other people have the same strengths?"

I thought about it. The whole point of strengths thinking is that we need each other to accomplish the tasks that are bigger than us.

Nehemiah picked up my thoughts: "And there is no way I could rebuild the wall by myself, every rock, every gate. So do what *you* know how to do. That's what I did. I knew how to drill down and identify the problem, identify a plan, and tell the people that they wouldn't be disgraced any more. I gave them hope. It's what leaders do. Go back and read my conversation with the people when I first got to Jerusalem. I said 'Come, let us rebuild the wall of Jerusalem, and we will

---

2. StrengthsFinder is an assessment to help you identify your top five strengths out of a list of thirty. I use the instrument regularly for team-building. Learn more at www.strengthsfinder.com.

no longer be in disgrace.'³ They felt disgraced. That's why I told them it would stop.

"Rather than focusing on the whole list, start looking for the things on the list that you can do and consider how those things might help the people already on the ground, the people who are aware of the problem and just need help to start.

"One last thing. In my case, they needed to know that God hadn't forgotten them. You might want to include that in what you are saying to the people around you. They might need to be reminded that God is involved."

But something bothered me. "How was God's involvement so clear to you?"

He smiled. "Remember that four-month prayer? Remember the king story? The fact that I was standing in Jerusalem at all was pretty clear evidence to me that God was involved. That's why 'I also told them about the gracious hand of my God on me and what the king had said to me.'"⁴

"Okay. I get it. Different people have different gifts and leaders have to lead. But why did you have to tell us by making us read this list?"

He walked upstairs to the kitchen and turned on the stove. It was time to switch to tea.

As he walked back into the office he said, **"Lesson three: Every worker's story needs to be told."**

"As we already said, you think that chapter 3 is a chapter.

3. Nehemiah 2:17.
4. Nehemiah 2:18

For me, it was the chart from the wall of the construction trailer, helping us know who was doing what. After the wall was built, I rolled it up and saved it. I wanted to remember that time. And when I wrote out my memoir, I put it here because it was an important list to keep.

"All of those people were people. All of those people worked. All of us were real people who had real stories about our work. There were people from inside and outside, there were people from every class of our culture. The religious people worked. The nobles worked–well, some of them. Families worked together. Neighborhoods. This was an amazing project. Eliashib. The men of Jericho who came down. Zaccur. Shallum's daughters.[5]"

I was losing him. He was so excited about the people. Name after name, and with every name it was clear that he knew these people and that he cared. It was clear that he had led them with his heart. No wonder he kept the list.

The teakettle was whistling. I coughed. He stopped. He went upstairs. When he came back, he was calmer.

I said, "What was that about the nobles?"

"You noticed. Good. That's **Lesson four: Not everyone is going to work the same way.**

"I know you." he said. "You want to give everyone a chance. But at some point, you need to be clear that some people help, some people help particularly well, and some people don't help at all. Pointing that out helps everyone.

"The nobles of Tekoa were particularly rude.[6] They were

5. Nehemiah 3:12.
6. Nehemiah 3:5.

unwilling to set aside their arrogance and follow competent builders. It's part of that point about different gifts. When you have a construction manager, a leader should see that and follow that. The leaders from Tekoa didn't."

I raised my hand. "You know, I was looking on a map for Tekoa. I noticed that it was southeast of the city. Is it possible that the rulers were willing to work on the section of the wall nearest them but that they didn't want to travel all the way across to the northwest side of the city? Because I noticed that the *men* of Tekoa worked in both places."

Nehemiah shrugged. "They were good workers. We assigned the best people to the places where we needed skill. I'm not interested in explaining why the nobles resisted our directions, it's enough to know that they did." Nehemiah smiled. "On the other hand, Baruch, Zabbia's son, did a great job. And it was worth noting.[7]

"And one last note here. When you look at the map of the city, some people and teams completed long sections. Others did short sections. That's because in some places the wall was damaged a little. In other places the wall was destroyed. Some people have the capacity to do lots of work. Others have the capacity to do a little. Let them do what they can do. And celebrate it."

He looked at me, looked at his tea, and said, "I need to finish up. Here's **Lesson five: Most people work hardest on what's closest to their heart.**

"Some people can work anywhere. But sometimes peo-

---

7. Nehemiah 3:20.

ple work best when they are repairing the part of the wall closest to home, closest to family. When we were facing the threat of attack, I moved people to be near their families, close to their homes. It gave them an added motivation to work hard."

"But isn't that being too easy on people?" I asked. It seemed to me that we should all work as hard as we can on everything.

"For me, for my brothers, for the soldiers that the king sent with me, you are correct," Nehemiah said. "It's our job. But these people weren't builders, they weren't soldiers, they weren't leaders. They were merchants and farmers, some from outside the walls, some from inside.

"Making them commute too far, making them care too much, isn't fair. So show people how the work relates to their family, and let them work close to home. It still counts. It still builds the wall."

I raised my hand. "Some of your workers were a little sloppy."

"What do you mean?"

"There's been some work looking for your wall. And the archaeologists have found a section of wall that looks a little uneven, a little amateurish. It looks like some people who were merchants and farmers were working on the wall."[8]

8. Eilat Mazar. "The wall that Nehemiah built." Accessed July 13, 2013
   http://www.dts.edu/download/other/ccl/
   CCL%20Leaderboard%20-%20Meeting%202%20-%20BAR%20Article.pdf

Nehemiah shrugged. "What did you expect? I made it up?"

I went back to his point. "You mean helping someone lead their own family matters? Working on only part of a larger project matters? Working without a sense of the bigger vision matters?"

"Absolutely," Nehemiah said. "God gave me the big vision. My job was to let people work on their parts and connect that to the big vision. And help you do the same. I hope that helps."

And he was gone.

I was left to summarize. And I think he said:

Give people permission to do what they know how to do. Give them hope in knowing that God cares about what they do. Give them a personal connection. Give them attention. Give them room to fail. And to succeed.

6

FACING THE RESISTANCE OF ENEMIES

Nehemiah 4

Nehemiah suggested we go out to the garage. When I opened the door, it didn't look at all like our garage, the garage always on the other side of that door. I mean, it was the same workbench my dad had made, the cold chisel that was my grandfather's; but somehow it looked different. More like a construction site.

"Take a seat," Nehemiah said, pointing to a limestone block. "I want to talk to you about conflict. You aren't very good at it."

He's right. I over-react, over-internalize. As I've been reading through his book, I've noticed over and over how Nehemiah seems to *respond* rather than *react*. I wanted to talk to him about it. Turned out, he wanted to talk to me.

And he wasn't much for conversation this morning. "I want to talk you through some of the resistance I've faced, the conflict I dealt with. Maybe you can learn something."

I got as comfortable as I could on a rock.

"You remember that I had a community meeting three days after I got to the city? It's when I said, 'The walls are ruined and the gates are burned. We are going to rebuild the walls.'"[1]

I smiled. Always reminding. "I remember."

"Shortly after that meeting, Sanballat, Tobiah, and Gershon found me. Sanballat was from a nearby town to the northwest. He was the biggest talker among the three. He had a hot temper. Gershon lived south. He was the muscle. Tobiah was an Ammonite, from the east, across the Jordan. He was … challenging. I'm not ready to talk about him yet. He was the most dangerous of the three because of his strong connections to the leadership. He was political.[2]

"They mocked us, accusing us of rebellion. It wasn't a serious threat, just an attempt to find out how serious I was.

"I let them know how serious I was. I told them that this was about God, that we were his servants, and that they had no right to be in this spiritual place."

Nehemiah dipped a stick in some pitch and wrote on the wall. I looked up the Aramaic. It said **"In the face of verbal challenge, respond with simple truth."**[3]

He continued. "A few days later, after we started work-

1. Nehemiah 2:17-18.
2. There is more on Tobiah in Chapter 18.
3. Nehemiah 2:19-20.

ing, they moved to a new level. Now that we were making real progress, we heard that they were starting to get nervous. They realized that I was serious about rebuilding these walls. It made Sanballat mad. So he started fussing to his cronies when they sat around the campfires.

"I knew that I could wait. The bluster was just that. To do anything would only waste resources and distract the crews. So instead of responding, I let everyone keep working. I did, however, talk to God.

'The tables are turned, God. We are doing your work this time, not ignoring you. So do to them what was done to us when we disobeyed you. Let them be hauled away to captivity. Let them have justice in your sight.'[4]

"I know it sounds rough, but I decided to trust God to work." He grabbed his stick again. **"In the face of insults, pray."**[5]

He refilled his mug. I realized that there was a coffee pot on this construction site. I got a mug, too. It tasted like it had been setting on the burner for centuries.

"Our adversaries kept getting madder. They started to make plans to attack us. But we needed to keep rebuilding the walls. Responding to the taunting and plotting wasn't worth stopping to fight. So this time I did two things. I prayed. And I posted a guard. In case they actually, accidentally, acted."

4. *My paraphrase of Nehemiah 2:20.*
5. *Nehemiah 4:1-5.*

He wrote the third lesson on the wall: "In the face of threats, pray and post a guard."[6]

Nehemiah walked across the stony ground and looked out across the city. I hadn't realized that we were on a hill, outside Jerusalem. Or at least that's what it looked like.

Staring at the city, he started talking again.

"The next time I had to deal with the boys, the problem was more serious. You may not have realized that I was listening closely to all the chatter. There was a structure to the way reports came to me. At this point, a month into the project, I was getting three streams of information.

"From the leaders who were working closely with the people, we started hearing that the adrenaline was wearing off.[7] They'd been working hard for several weeks, harder than they had ever worked in their lives. I knew that when you are leading people, the time in the middle is rough. They don't have the excitement of starting. They don't have the passion of seeing the end in sight. They are tired and the piles of rubble still seem huge.

"Then we started hearing from our enemies again.[8] This time, they were talking about being able to come through gaps in the wall and attack us. They had all the advantage. They knew the city. There were no gates. Their plans made sense.

"We had heard all this before, but this time it was a little more serious. The people who lived out in the villages could

6. Nehemiah 4:6-9.
7. Nehemiah 4:10.
8. Nehemiah 4:11.

see that the plans were more detailed. Sanballat, Tobiah, and Gershon were practicing. They were setting up camp. When people came to work each day, we got report after report giving us warnings.[9]

"So this time, we were facing a combination of worn-out workers and a credible threat. I decided that we needed to be more proactive. I looked at the progress we had made. Because some of the wall had been damaged less, the work had gone faster. But the places where there had been attacks in the past, those places where the rubble was worst, the work was slower. If you remember back to the list of all the people clustered in small areas, they were working in these areas. I moved people so that they were with their families; they were by the part of the wall that protected them most.

"After I made these arrangements of people, I walked around the city to see how we were doing. And then I got the leadership together. It was time for a speech. It was time for a *simple* speech.

1. Don't be afraid of them.
2. You are working for God.
3. When you fight, fight for the people you love.

"This was a life and death turning point. At those moments people need spiritual truth and they need personal connection."

I interrupted. "And it worked. They backed off. You did it."

Nehemiah shook his head. "What we all did is give God

9. Nehemiah 4:12.

credit for frustrating it. It wasn't my skill. If I hadn't been aware of our people, if we hadn't had people from our side who heard about the plans, if our enemies had been more about strategy and less about bluster, they could have taken us."

Nehemiah stood silent, watching the history as if he could feel the threat. I picked up his stick. I think I understood the lesson. "In the face of an opposition it's mobilizing, implement a clear plan, which includes meaningful action, leadership strategy and reminding the people of the purpose."[10]

He looked at what I had written.

"That's good. A little long, but that's what we did. And it worked. But after that scare, it was clear that we needed a strong defensive presence. God had never given me the freedom to go on the offense. This work wasn't about defeating *them*, it was about rebuilding *us*. So we kept rebuilding. But now I divided my people into two groups. One group kept working. The other stood guard. The people who were working were on guard as well. We had them carry swords when they were carrying lumber. On one hand, it slowed people down. On the other, everyone was way more focused. They were clearly engaged in the work. They looked for the shortest distances to carry materials, to help each other. They watched each others' backs. They weren't tempted to sit, resting in the valley. Everyone was alert and engaged.

10. Nehemiah 4:10-15.

"And my men and my brother and I did the best we could to let everyone know that we were aware. We were the first ones on the job. We were the last ones to bed. We had coffee ready when the crew got up. If anyone wondered whether the leaders cared, they only had to listen for the scrape of our swords on the rocks by the latrine."

"So what's the last lesson?" he asked.

"Try this," I said. **"For long-term protection, lay out a clear defense that is sustainable. It gives the people something at their back so they can go about the work."**[11]

"That works," Nehemiah said. "Now go back home."

"But was that the end of the challenges? I thought they kept harassing you."

"They did," he said. "But I'm tired and so are you. Learn these lessons about active resistance and I'll tell you about the sneaky kind sometime later. But next time we talk, I want to talk about a more challenging kind of resistance."

I walked back through the door into our family room. When I looked over my shoulder to ask if he wanted more coffee, he was gone. And the shelves with piles of my life were back.

11. Nehemiah 4:16-23.

7

FACING THE RESISTANCE OF FRIENDS

Nehemiah 5

Today there was pie. Nehemiah and I shared the leftover pie (pumpkin for him, apple for me), sipped coffee, and started talking about unexpected resistance.

"What happens when the people you are leading start whining?" I asked. Not that I was facing that myself at the moment.

"What makes you think they are whining?" he asked.

"Look at what happened to you in the middle of the building project. Some of the families started to complain. It was bad enough to have the outsiders attacking, but now your own people were complaining."

"What makes you think they were complaining?" he said. He raised his hand to stop my response. "There was an outcry, but they weren't complaining. They were speaking truth. For the first time in years they finally had someone they trusted as a leader, and they were speaking truth."

I took another bite of pie.

"The people around Jerusalem had the same mixture of economic and social classes that you find around you. When the Babylonians finally dragged us away, the people they left were poor people, shepherds and farmers.[1] For years they lived as best they could off the land. Up around Samaria, some of them married the people the Babylonians had brought in.[2] Some did their best to stay loyal to God. And then, for the past fifty years, people had been returning from Babylon. Some of them came for their own reasons. Some came specifically to rebuild the temple.

"As a result, we had farmers and merchants and nobles and Levites, Jews and Samaritans and distant relatives like the Ammonites, people brought in from other parts of the world and people who descended from the people who had been in the land when Joshua led the Israelites into the

---

1. For example, we read that "Nebuzaradan the commander of the guard carried into exile the people who remained in the city, along with the rest of the populace and those who had deserted to the king of Babylon. *But the commander left behind some of the poorest people of the land to work the vineyards and fields.*" 2 Kings 25:11-12 NIV (italics mine).

2. The Samaritan story extends into stories that Jesus told. It starts in 2 Kings 17:24: "The king of Assyria brought people from Babylon, Kuthah, Avva, Hamath and Sepharvaim and settled them in the towns of Samaria to replace the Israelites. They took over Samaria and lived in its towns." The rest of that chapter describes the mixing of the religions of their homelands with following the God of Israel. By the time of Jesus, the Israelites who had returned from exile (including any of Nehemiah's family) were at odds with the Samaritans who had blended religions.

Promised Land." Nehemiah picked up his pie for another bite.

I said, "I'm guessing that some people had plenty of resources and some didn't. That always happens with people. But how did that cause problems for you?"

He wiped his chin. "Everyone had to feed their families; not everyone had enough food, especially those who returned from the exile. And these people who had grown up in exile had finally gotten to the homeland and wanted to have families. People mortgaged what property they had to buy food. After awhile, these people who had mortgaged their land faced the tax collectors. But whatever they raised in crops was going to the note-holders, and they *still* had to pay for food."

I thought about it. "It was like the foreclosure crisis is now. People are upside down on their mortgages," I said. "And those people are really scared."

"That's it exactly," Nehemiah answered. "But it got worse. People had to get money somehow, so they sent their children out to work. We didn't have child labor laws. So it looked a lot more like slavery. Or worse. It was a loop. You borrow money to buy food. You borrow more money to pay taxes. And the only way you can pay all that interest is to send your kids to work for the lender."

I stopped him. "And then you came on the scene."

"Yes," Nehemiah said. "When I came as the governor, there was finally a Jewish leader in Jerusalem. So it wasn't that they were mad at me or complaining without reason. They realized that someone cared."

"So the tension I run into might be a compliment more than a complaint?" I asked. "And the whining may be a legitimate cry for justice?"

"Absolutely. Parents came to me and started telling me what was happening. I heard story after story of people with resources taking advantage of parents without resources.

"Then I began seeing an aggravating pattern. Sometimes people would borrow from the non-Jewish merchants and have to send their kids into service.[3] When other Jews had resources, they would redeem the kids. They wanted our kids to grow up with our culture. Then I heard about Jewish merchants who would loan money for food, who would then have kids coming into their service, and who would then receive some of the redemption money.[4] These merchants were taking advantage of the community."

I asked, "I'm guessing that they figured that if someone was going to get interest, it might as well stay in the family?"

Nehemiah set his mug down. It hit harder than I expected. "But God said not to do that. It's what was called

3. The way the law was written, poor Jews might need to borrow from non-Jewish people living in the land. In that case, Jewish family members had by law the right to redeem those who were in service. (See Leviticus 25:47-55.) What isn't clear is whether you could send your children into service or if this is because things were really difficult for the poor people in Nehemiah's time.

4. The redemption model only applied to non-Jews. You couldn't charge interest like this to your own people. The redemption model didn't apply. What did apply was a law that said "if Jews work for you, treat them as hired hands." (Leviticus 25:39-43) In another place, "When they have fulfilled their agreed time of service, send them on their way with a share of the profits you made with their help." Deuteronomy 15:12-18.

usury, charging family for what should be part of what we do for each other, because it all comes from God anyway."

"Wait, what? You are making this be a big spiritual thing?

Nehemiah sighed. "It *is* a spiritual thing. It's *all* spiritual."

He took a deep breath. I shuddered. I remembered that when Nehemiah stopped to think, it often was because he was getting angry, and he wanted to respond rather than react.

He spoke quietly. "It's not you. It's the whole big story. Our Jewishness was a story. I had spent the last eight months meditating on the story as I was praying and planning and starting to work.

"When Moses talked about coming into the land, way back while we were still wanderers, he gave us instructions about what to do with the very first crop we got.[5] People were to put the first grain they harvested into a basket and take it to the priest. They were to say to the priest, each of them, 'My father was a wandering Aramean. His family went to Egypt. They had babies and became a great nation and were used and then abused by the Egyptians. We called out to God, who heard us, rescued us, and brought us to this land. This food is the first food I raised on the land God gave me. And I'm giving it to God to help me remember.'

"The reason God forbade charging interest to family is because he was giving us resources to care for each other. It

---

5. Deuteronomy 26:1-11.

came from God. People forgot the story. And some people forgot that our identity was rooted in God's relationship to us."

I held up my hand. "So the simplest thing would have been to simply give people food rather than the whole elaborate borrowing and interest, right?"

"Exactly. Not borrowing money for food meant that people would have been able to pay taxes without selling their kids into slavery.[6] When you are a family, you share. You have to work, but you share.[7] When you start looking at people as business, the family is over. And as someone who had given up his entire life for the sake of the family, the people, I was furious."

Even though I already knew the answer, I asked, "So what did you do?" I wanted a summary.

"Six simple steps," Nehemiah said.

"First, **I took a very deep breath.** I knew I could be violent if I wasn't careful.[8]

"Second, **I confronted the leaders.** That's where the problem started, with their permissiveness.[9]

---

6. The idea of usury is mentioned in Deuteronomy 23:19-20 and Exodus 22:25-27.

7. This is about family: "If any of your fellow Israelites become poor and are unable to support themselves among you, help them as you would a foreigner and stranger, so they can continue to live among you. Do not take interest or any profit from them, but fear your God, so that they may continue to live among you. You must not lend them money at interest or sell them food at a profit. I am the Lord your God, who brought you out of Egypt to give you the land of Canaan and to be your God." Leviticus 25:35-38 See also Deuteronomy 15:7-11 for the image of being open-handed toward the family.

8. Nehemiah 5:6-7.

9. Nehemiah 5:7.

"Third, I called everyone together and clearly outlined the problem.[10]"

I interrupted. "And they agreed, right?"

"Absolutely. How could they argue, especially in front of the parents of the kids.

"Fourth, I explained what we all could do, looking to the Bible for support.[11]"

I interrupted again. "You told people to return the land that had been mortgaged, to just eliminate the mortgages. Wasn't that what God had commanded to happen every seven years anyway?"[12]

"Yes it was. What I knew was that the Sabbath year that God had commanded, where mortgages were eliminated, was important for two reasons. First, God had commanded it to remind us that the land had been given to us by God. And second, disobeying this command had been part of the reason for the exile. I was pretty sure I didn't want to be part of anything that would send us back to exile."

I got Nehemiah back on track. "Number five?"

"Fifth, I brought the leaders together and had them make a public commitment.[13] And then sixth, I made the promises visual.[14]"

"I loved that," I said. "Shaking the crumbs out of your robe was visible to the whole crowd. Everyone knew the promise. Everyone knew the results of disobedience."

10. Nehemiah 5:7-10.
11. Nehemiah 5:10-12.
12. Deuteronomy 15:1-6.
13. Nehemiah 5:12.
14. Nehemiah 5:13.

Nehemiah stood up and shook the pie crumbs off his lap. "God doesn't have surprises. He gives plenty of warning, lots of visuals, clear opportunities to obey. In fact, our whole lives were a visual for you."

And he was gone.

I started thinking through some of the comments people have made to me. I thought it was whining. I started wondering whether I'd been listening closely enough.

8

FACING RESISTANCE
FROM YOURSELF

Nehemiah 6

Nehemiah isn't a shy person, but he is a little hesitant to talk about his commitment. So he's letting me write this chapter without him.

After trying threats, Nehemiah's enemies tried tricks. "Come out to meet us," they said. "We just want to talk." Nehemiah knew that this was a trap.

And so, of course, he didn't go. But as he responded, his focus wasn't on the trap. His focus was on the task at hand.

"I am doing a great work and I cannot come down. Why should the work stop while I leave it and come down to you?"[1]

Every time I read those words, I want to stand up in respect. Or fall down, heart convicted.

1. *Nehemiah 6:3.*

Say that out loud. "I am doing a great work." Doesn't that give you chills? Doesn't that make you wish you could say that about what you are doing?

Nehemiah was rebuilding walls around "The City of God." He had come 900 miles to do this work. He had prayed and planned and risked his life. He was completely committed to this project. It mattered.

Maybe you are doing something that matters, though you don't see it that way. Maybe you are rebuilding the walls of protection for children whose lives have been wrecked. Maybe you are rebuilding your own life. Maybe you are just starting to build a foundation of following Jesus.

Go ahead. Say it again. "I am doing a great work."

"I cannot come down."

Nehemiah knew better than many of us that sticking to the work means not engaging in distractions. It means responding to critics by reminding them of the significance of the work we are doing and then going back to that work. It means using this same response (e.g. "I can't come down") over and over and over. (Four times for Nehemiah in this story).

When we understand that the work we are doing is great, then we are less likely to be involved in doing things that are merely good. That's true even if those good things aren't traps like the distractions Nehemiah was facing.

Except, the things around us could be traps.

I wonder if you are like me. We have a great work we want to do. Before we start, we check to see what's happening in the world. We look at the clock and discover that five or fifteen or fifty minutes have gone by. We have read interesting things. We have learned much, perhaps. But we have made no progress on our "great work." So we start again. When we come to a hard part, while we are thinking, we check to see what's happening. Our fear of missing out (FOMO) is so intense that we miss out on the important work we could do.

You know what I mean?

Listen. Everyone who was working with Nehemiah, every person hauling bricks, every person standing guard, every person involved was part of this "great work." Raising kids, doing your job well, rebuilding relationships or communities can all be "great works."

When you believe the work you are called to is great, it's easier to say "I can't come down."

"Why should the work stop?"

We hear all the time about not thinking of yourself too highly, of learning to be humble and being part of a team. I agree. But I also am learning much from Nehemiah about accepting the responsibility of taking responsibility. Though Nehemiah was not indispensable, he was the heartbeat of this project, this great work. That was his part of this project, to keep it happening.

- Nehemiah's heart was the one broken about the broken walls of Jerusalem.
- Nehemiah risked his career to enlist the king's help.
- Nehemiah traveled 900 miles by horse and foot.
- Nehemiah surveyed the damage himself.

- Nehemiah rallied the residents to start rebuilding these walls.
- Nehemiah planned work strategy and defensive strategy and morale strategy and prayer strategy.
- Nehemiah was everywhere during the project.

Being an effective leader–and being a follower of Jesus means that you care enough about the work you are assigned to do that you don't follow rabbit trails. While you are on duty, you are on duty. You never let yourself walk away while you are in the middle of a project where you hold the vision and you care about the outcome and you are passionately concerned about protecting the hands and hearts of the rest of the team. You accept the significance of your leadership because you understand that serving means owning up.

So what makes a work great? At this midpoint of Nehemiah's story, that is a wonderful question.

Here are some suggestions:

- **Something about it makes you weep.** When Nehemiah hears about the condition of the walls of the city of God, it breaks his heart.
- **It's bigger than you.** Hugely so. Rebuilding a city? Putting wells in every village in a country in Africa? No homeless children in your community? One particular person in your neighborhood knowing that they are listened to and loved?
- **You have to take lots of small steps that don't seem like they will get you anywhere.** Each stone that

Nehemiah's crew moved seemed insignificant compared to a two-mile city wall. But each stone needed to be moved.

- **Doing the work transforms you.** Nehemiah was a seasoned leader when this was done.
- **God calls you to do it.** I know. This one can creep people out. But Nehemiah clearly believed that God was giving him this work. We don't always understand the mechanics of God's calling. And we have clear and tragic examples of people who attached the name of God to their own projects. But Nehemiah was clearly responding to the direction that God had given him.
- It matters enough that you ache when you can't accomplish it quickly enough, and it's big enough that you can't accomplish it quickly enough. Every day working on a great project excites you, drains you and (some days) blesses you.
- **It is not about you.** This is tough. A great work is about others, not about you. So my weight loss is great, but it isn't a great work.
- **It takes so long that you can't do it in a day, but the choices of each day matter in whether you can get it done.** Every day you have to choose to take those steps we mentioned earlier. Every single day.
- **You may not know anything about how to do the work.** It may have nothing to do with your job. In fact, it may cause you to leave your job or may turn into a job.

- You cannot *not* do it.

Maybe you've been thinking about great work. Maybe you've been looking at the work in front of you and thinking, "It's well and good to talk about Nehemiah. Of course his work was great. It was God's work."

That's what we see now. That's what we see through Nehemiah's eyes. Other eyes would see differently.

If we were standing next to Nehemiah, about 30 miles from the Mediterranean looking east, we would have been reminded of the black-and-white photos we've seen of bombed cities. Walls in places, gaps in others. Whatever wood is left where gates once were is charred and worm-eaten. Beautiful houses have lost their back walls. The houses least touched, the walls least broken, are in the poorer parts of town, as if they weren't worth a warrior's notice.

"A fox would topple this wall" is what one skeptic said during the rebuilding process, reminding us that animals have been running this rubble for decades.[2]

This "great work" of Nehemiah's is a rubbish pile, 900 miles from the center of power, in the worthless wilderness between Greece and Persia. This "great work" is rebuilding the capital of a two-tribe nation, the last remnant of the twelve tribes of Israel. This "great work" was great only because Nehemiah believed it was. Nehemiah and God.

Nehemiah and God and the people. These were people who had been unwilling subjects of a distant-feeling King

---

2. That was Tobiah, as recorded in Nehemiah 4:3.

(God) until they ended up as unwilling subjects of a distant human king. Now that Nehemiah was here to give God-inspired hope, they were hopeful and energetic.

But there was still the reality of the rubble.

When you look at the work that God has in front of you, whether writing or children or ashes or dust, it may not appear great. But appearances deceive.

9

CELEBRATION AND GRIEF

Nehemiah 7:73-8:11

I was reading a story at the beginning of chapter 8 of *Nehemiah*.

"Why were the people crying?" I asked Nehemiah.

He looked up, a little confused. He looked like he had been napping.

"I read that the people had gathered and you all heard Ezra read the law and they started crying.[1] Why? Was it exhaustion?"

"Who wouldn't have cried?" he asked, as if my question made no sense to him. His tone told me that his apparent confusion about my question wasn't because of sleep-induced fogginess. "You would have been crying, too."

His last statement told me nothing. I'm sentimental. I cry all the time.

1. Nehemiah 8:9.

"This wasn't about being sentimental," he said, as if reading my thoughts. "If you read the story carefully, you'll see that they weren't crying the way you cry about a melancholy commercial for a greeting card company. They were grieving. The chest-crushing, leg-weakening, breath-stopping realization you have when you realize how much you hurt someone you love. Which is why I stopped them."

"But why stop them?" I said. "I mean, didn't they deserve to grieve? You, yourself, had talked with God about the sin of, how did you say it, 'your ancestors and your family and you.'"[2]

I looked down at my Bible. Nehemiah's silence somehow filled the room. I looked up.

His face looked old, older than I had ever noticed. We talk of people feeling drained, and as I looked at Nehemiah, I suddenly understood the phrase.

When he finally spoke, his voice was fragile.

"God wanted a people, not revenge."

I walked to the kitchen to get him water. And to make myself tea. I needed the routine of heating water and steeping the leaves. I needed to be ready to listen.

When I got back to my office, Nehemiah had recovered a bit of his poise.

"Sit down," he said gently. "Let me tell you the story. But it will take time. This one morning was a gathering of so many threads of so many lives that is it worth the waiting.

---

2. This is in Nehemiah's prayer in Nehemiah 1:6.

Please humor an old man. I'll do my best to lay these threads out simply.

"We completed the wall in 52 days. I believe you read that."[3]

I nodded.

"It wasn't *finished*, of course. There was still work to be done. We wouldn't be able to do the dedication, with a walk on top of the walls, for awhile.[4] But there was an unbroken wall around Jerusalem for the first time in generations. We could breathe easier."

"The effect on your enemies must have been significant," I said.

"It was," he agreed. "The political enemies, like Tobiah, were not stopped. Physical walls mean nothing to schemers. But people who depend on strength, who never believed we would do this great work, were impressed. And because we had been so clear that God had given us this work, they understood that God must have helped us complete it.[5]

"With the wall completed this far, we let workers go back to their villages. Some had been staying in Jerusalem for the last month of work. After sunrise to sunset commitment, everyone needed a break."

"But who was protecting the city?" I said.

"Well, first there were still some people living in the city. Remember the people who had been working on the

3. Nehemiah 6:15.
4. Nehemiah 12:27-43.
5. Nehemiah 6:16. We never hear about Sanballat and Geshem again in this book, though Sanballat's son-in-law was mentioned years later.

wall in front of their houses? And then there were people who had come with me from Susa, like my brother and some guards. They were always my first line of defense. And third, with a wall in place, some people were able to do the work they'd been assigned to do. Hanahiah, for example, had been guarding the temple grounds. Now that the walls of the city were set, he could oversee the whole city with his people.[6] In two months, we had seen the real character of many people. He was more faithful than most.

"After a week, it was time to come back together. The people felt a need to hear from God. They asked Ezra to read. By a curious work of timing, a week or so after we finished the wall was the beginning of the seventh month, Tishrei. It was time for a celebration."

I interrupted. "Why the seventh month? Ezra talks about a gathering on that date, too, decades before this.[7] But what was special about this month?"

Nehemiah was patient. "Every kingdom, every empire, seems to have different ways of marking time. Because of my work as cupbearer, I was used to many calendars. Often, the beginning of a dynasty is the beginning of the new year. In fact, for our people, Passover had been the start of the civil year.

"But, we also have the religious year. And the religious year started on the first day of the seventh month, Tishrei. God told Moses to set it aside to gather, to blow trumpets, to not work, and to offer sacrifice. It was a simple celebration.

6. Nehemiah 7:2.
7. Ezra 3:1.

Moses called it the Feast of Trumpets.[8] You may know it as Rosh Hashanah."

"You mean, Jewish New Year?" I said. I got excited. "Did you get the appropriateness? That you were getting to start the process of rebuilding the people as a nation so soon after rebuilding the wall? That you got started at the beginning of the year was pretty amazing."

Nehemiah shrugged slightly. "We're not always as in control of the seasons and timing in our lives as we would like to think." He took a sip of water and looked at the sun. It looked like gold through the trees outside the west window of my office. "May I resume my story?"

I nodded, smiling at his formality.

"Many people came to Jerusalem for that day. There was a sense of excitement. Men who had come in from the villages during the building process brought their wives and families. It was the first time many people had seen the finished wall.

"We built a platform by the Water Gate, on the east side of the city. It was an open place, outside the new wall we had built, but inside the older wall. Ezra was just as excited as anyone. He had been preparing for this day his whole life."

"What do you mean?" I asked. "And why is Ezra suddenly showing up here?" I had been doing some reading. Ezra was another person who had come from Babylon to Jerusalem at the direction of the king. Some scholars say he arrived in Jerusalem several years before Nehemiah, oth-

8. This feast is described in Leviticus 23:23-25 and Numbers 29:1-6.

ers say he came during Nehemiah's time. One of the timing questions about the writing of *Nehemiah* is that Ezra appears so arbitrarily after the work is done.

"I never had need to mention him before. He wasn't much of a builder. He was what you might call 'spiritual'. He had devoted his life to three things: studying the law, obeying the law, and teaching the law.[9] His reputation for living out the law was humbling to me. When he saw disobedience, his response was to spend whole days in tears before God.

"So back to that day. In the pale light before dawn, several of the nobles and leaders of the people came up onto the platform."

"Who were they?" I asked. "Were they the religious leaders or the politicians or who?"

"You wouldn't know them," he said. "Not most of them. A couple were leaders who had worked on the wall. But they mattered to the people who were watching.

"At sunrise, a ram's horn trumpet sounded. After using it to warn the people of attack, it was a relief to have it call people to God.[10] As the sun came over the shoulder of the Mount of Olives, Ezra climbed up the steps onto the platform carrying the scroll. He found his place in the center of the line of leaders. He started to read. The crowd fell silent:

'Sh'ma Yis'ra'eil Adonai Eloheinu Adonai echa'"

9. Ezra 7:9-10.
10. Nehemiah 4:18.

My breath stopped as Nehemiah said the ancient words, eyes closed, slowly standing to his feet. For a moment, he wasn't here with me anymore. He was there, hearing Ezra.

"Wait," I blurted out. Nehemiah opened one eye. "I know that, somehow. It sounds familiar. Shema, right? *The Shema?*"

Nehemiah opened the other eye. "It's why we all got quiet. *Sh'ma* is simply the ancient Hebrew word for 'Hear.'"

"I know," I said impatiently. "But I know that, according to Jesus, it's the beginning of the most important commandment. 'Hear, O Israel, the Lord is our God. The Lord is one.'"

Nehemiah joined me as I spoke: "'Love the Lord your God with all your heart and with all your soul and with all your strength.'"

"That's what Ezra read?" I sat back, stunned.

"What did you think he read?" Nehemiah said. "We wrote it right into the text you've been reading:

They told Ezra the teacher of the Law to bring out the Book of the Law of Moses, which the Lord had commanded for Israel.[II]

"It was the book of the law, the teaching that God gave Moses. It made the most sense on this day to read what you call Deuteronomy, the best summary Moses gave of the law. And where else to start but with the words that everyone

---

II. *Nehemiah* 8:1

73

knew, that every child learned as soon as we learned anything: 'Hear, O Israel.'

"But very quickly, most people lost track of what Ezra was reading. They didn't know Hebrew. We didn't know Hebrew, beyond a few prayers. Centuries before, in the time of Hezekiah, the diplomats of Judah learned Aramaic as the language of international trade.[12] It was the language of commerce, the language of trade, the language of government. By 500 BC, before I was born, Aramaic had become the official language of Persia. During the time of exile, those of us in Babylon learned it to survive. The people left in Jerusalem learned it to speak to the outsiders who had been brought in. By now, everyone spoke Aramaic as their first language and only a few spoke Hebrew."[13]

"And so, as Ezra read the law, we recognized words or phrases, but we were missing so much. Or we would have if it hadn't been for the Levites. They spoke Hebrew *and* Aramaic. Ezra did as well. His work as a scribe for the Persians had made him very fluent.

"As Ezra read, thirteen of the Levites moved through the crowd. They would stop near a family group and translate the words of Moses, read by Ezra in Hebrew, into the language of the people.[14]

---

12. In 2 Kings 18, Assyrian invaders spoke Hebrew when they stood before the city gates and threatened invasion. The leaders asked them to switch to Aramaic, since that was the appropriate diplomatic approach. "But the commander replied, 'Was it only to your master and you that my master sent me to say these things, and not to the people sitting on the wall—who, like you, will have to eat their own excrement and drink their own urine?'(2 Kings 18:27.)

13. And years later, some of the children would be speaking the languages of their non-Jewish mothers.

"It was an awesome sight. The people standing silent, the leaders listening, Ezra reading, the Levites moving around explaining, translating. You could see the waves of understanding spreading around the Levites like rings around water drops."

I let Nehemiah enjoy the moment. But talking about the scene, as helpful as it was, didn't answer my question. After a bit, I asked again. "So why were the people crying?"

Nehemiah closed his eyes and shook his head to clear it. He looked out the window which was now dark blue, with a trace of pink. "It's too late tonight," he said. "Meet me here in the morning."

And he was gone.

---

14. Eugene Peterson makes the argument that the Levites were translators on this day, though the kind of translators that explain or paraphrase. It's not teaching what to do, it's more teaching what it says. See Peterson, *Eat This Book*. Grand Rapids: Eerdmans, 2006, pp. 125-126.

10

NEHEMIAH'S ANSWERED PRAYER

Nehemiah 7:73-8:11

When I came down at 6 the next morning, Nehemiah was waiting for me. But he did let me get my coffee.

I yawned. "Okay, one more time. Why were they cry-ing?"

Nehemiah shook his head. "That's not the right ques-tion. The better question is, 'Why did I tell them to stop?'"

I shrugged. I didn't care which question, as long as I heard the story. "I'll play along," I said. "Why did you tell them to stop grieving?"

"Get comfortable," he said. "There are four reasons, but they aren't exactly bullet points. You are going to have to think."

Nehemiah started: "The first reason is the most simple. The first day of the seventh month was a day of feasting, not grieving. There were other times to mourn, to repent, to lament. This day was specified by God through Moses as a day to feast and not to work. God doesn't review our sins merely to make us sad, he forgives our sins to restore our relationship."

"What about the Day of Atonement?" I said. "It's one of those days of repenting. But I notice that you don't mention it at all in your discussion of what happened during this month."

Nehemiah was silent.

"I know that some people say that it could have happened up at the temple and not been recorded in this narrative. Others say that you couldn't be expected to do everything at the beginning of the nation building. But what do you say?"

Nehemiah was silent.

"Okay," I said, giving up. "Go ahead and tell your story the way you want to."

"This day was specified by God through Moses as a day to feast and not to work," Nehemiah said again. "It was important for the people to understand that God wants us to obey his commands to celebrate just as much as his commands to repent. I mentioned God's holiness as a reason to celebrate. I talked about being strengthened by the joy of the Lord. I wanted the people to have a quick and delightful opportunity to obey God."

"That makes sense," I said. "So what are more complicated reasons you told them not to grieve?"

Nehemiah took a sip from his mug. "The second reason was that we were living out the completion of the story

Moses had told. The text says that Ezra read the Book of the Law of Moses."

"That's a lot of reading," I said. "You know that there are several suggestions of what that meant. Did Ezra read the whole five books of Moses, the Pentateuch? You had five hours for reading. It's possible to read that much. Did he read some compilation of the law that he or someone else had assembled? I'm not sure which of those scholars is right. And you don't seem to be telling. But what makes the most sense to me is that the people heard at the very least the book of Deuteronomy, Moses' last words to the people."

Nehemiah shrugged. "Deuteronomy starts with a gathering of Jews, too. They are standing on the edge of the Promised Land. Before he dies, Moses wants to review what matters, to give the people he's been leading for forty years a clear picture of who they are as a people chosen by God. So Moses reviewed their history together, and generations later Ezra read it to us and the Levites explained it. Think through all the things that were in that story:

- Moses reminded them that 40 years before God sent them to take possession of the land he had promised to Abraham, Isaac and Jacob.[1]
- Moses reminded them that there were so many people needing direction that he had appointed leaders to help him.[2]
- When they got near the land, they sent spies who

1. Deuteronomy 1:8.
2. Deuteronomy 1:9-18. The longer story of Jethro and Moses is told in Exodus 18.

brought fear into their hearts, enough fear that the people disobeyed God.[3]

- So they wandered for forty years.[4]
- Near the end of the wandering, they came near Esau's descendants, the Edomites. They came near Lot's descendants, the Moabites and Ammonites. And God reminded them that though these weren't their own people, they were relatives of the promise and so he took care of them.[5]
- Moses tells them that because of his sin, he can't enter the Promised Land."[6]

I interrupted: "So in the first few chapters of Deuteronomy, they learn that God is fiercely protective of his own and committed to helping them learn to obey."

"Right," Nehemiah answered. "It is a simple review of a difficult time they shared. Then Moses turns to the future.

- Moses talks about learning the Law through daily review and teaching and the way God gave the Law and the way God didn't destroy them because he chose them and loves them.
- Then Moses reviews the Law, the Ten Commandments and more.[7]

---

3. Deuteronomy 1:22-33.
4. Deuteronomy 2:7.
5. Deuteronomy 2:16-22.
6. Deuteronomy 4:21-23. The full story is in Numbers 20:1-12. But it's possible that Moses hadn't told the people that he wasn't going into the land until this speech at the end of his life.
7. Deuteronomy 5-29.

- Moses tells them that the Law is close to them, in their mouths and in their hearts.[8]
- Moses tells them, "these are not just idle words for you, these are your life."[9]
- And Moses in very clear words gives them specific warnings: if God's people obey him, he will care for them, but if they disobey, they will feel the pain of feeling abandoned by God (though he won't abandon them). And if they repent, he will restore them."[10]

I leaned forward. "So when the people listened to Ezra read Deuteronomy, they heard a review of the first exodus and arrival at the Promised Land. When they were grieving, they had just heard Moses' words:

> Even if you have been banished to the most distant land under the heavens, from there the Lord your God will gather you and bring you back. He will bring you to the land that belonged to your ancestors, and you will take possession of it.[11]

Nehemiah just nodded.

I looked right at him. "I'm beginning to understand the tears. The thoughtful ones would have realized that because they had just been brought back from the farthest land, it was clear that God told the truth about working with his

8. Deuteronomy 30:14.
9. Deuteronomy 32:47.
10. Deuteronomy 30.
11. *Deuteronomy 30:4-5.*

people. Apparently, God was willing to sacrifice his city for the sake of getting the attention of his people. But I also understand why you told them to celebrate. Moses had been proved right.

"And now, this idea of the farthest land. Symbolically, Babylon was the 'farthest land' for the Israelites. Right? Because as you traveled from Susa to Jerusalem, you retraced at least some of the steps of Abram."

Nehemiah nodded again. "That's the third part of this story. The story of Abram started in Ur, in what you call Iraq, between Baghdad and Kuwait. God took him to Canaan, where he was promised the land. Then God took his family to Egypt, where they grew to be a nation. Then God rescued them and fulfilled his promise to Abraham, giving them the Promised Land. And then we spent a thousand years obeying and disobeying and obeying and disobeying until it was clear that we couldn't live as God's people. So we were taken to exile. Some of us went as far as Susa, which was east of Ur, further from Jerusalem than where Abram had started.[12]

"When we heard Ezra read from Deuteronomy that disobedience meant being scattered, we knew that God was serious. In the century and a half before this day, we had gone, as a people, back to where we were when Abraham

---

12. I first heard this idea in a series of lectures by John Goldingay. (John Goldingay. "The Prophets - Introduction." OT 502: The Prophets. Fuller Theological Seminary. Available from iTunes U. Released August 5 2009. Accessed November 4, 2013. Lecture.)

was first called. It was like a factory reset button. Everything went back to before there was an Israel."

"Except it wasn't," I said. "It wasn't a reset. God hadn't forgotten. Your four-month prayer in chapter one was taken straight from this story in Deuteronomy. You repented and you reminded God that even if your people were scattered, God would bring you back."

Nehemiah smiled, as big a smile as I had ever seen. "Exactly," he said. "This day was a complete answer to my prayer for a return. More than favor with the king, more than safe travel, more than a speedy rebuilding or deliverance from enemies, this moment answered my appeals to God. Standing as God's people, listening to God's promise of restoration to the city that we had just helped rebuild, I was overjoyed and humbled. This day was a specific answer to our specific prayer based on Moses's specific telling of God's specific promise. This was clear evidence that God answered our persistent prayer from months before."

Finally, I understood. I understood the deep grieving. But this was a new year, a new day, a new opportunity. God made this a feast day. Repentance doesn't mean continued groveling. It means living in freedom. And so they feasted. All of them at the celebration and even people who hadn't come. On this day, everyone had the opportunity to celebrate things being rebuilt.

I thanked Nehemiah for his patience with me. I don't think he heard me. He was still smiling, looking over my shoulder at a celebration I could only imagine.

LEARNING AND LIVING THE STORIES

Nehemiah 8:13-18

I wasn't sure what to say to Nehemiah this afternoon. The news of children being slaughtered this week was awful.[1] I mostly wanted to sit quietly and try to understand. He waited. I realized that he'd seen his own share of brutality and confusion and questions.

"Why did you tell so many stories?" I asked Nehemiah.

"I didn't," he said.

"But the whole book is a story. And I read about you telling stories all the time."

"Read it again," he said. "I'm not telling so many stories. I'm telling the same stories so many times."

"What's the difference?"

---

1. This was written one Sunday in 2012 after 29 children were murdered in a school in Connecticut. But it could have been written any time. There are always children being killed.

"There's a huge difference. If you tell too many stories, you may just start creating an appetite for novelty, an appetite for the next story. People want to hear Rob's story and then Megin's version of the story and then the story about Rob's response to Megin's story and how the kids reacted."

"Is that bad? I mean, assuming that it's a funny story and not about the time he broke his leg."

"It's not bad unless all you are ever doing is talking about people and their problems. It's so easy to slide into gossip. It's so easy to start feeding 24-hour news cycles."

I looked at him. "What do you know about the news?"

Nehemiah laughed. "I thought you read the book. Remember when people came to me ten times talking about the way Sanballat and Tobiah were plotting against us?[2] It was the main story on the early morning news for nearly two weeks. Every morning when people came in from their villages to work on the wall, I heard the news: 'You should have seen Sanballat's campfire last night. It was huge. And the war songs they were singing. I couldn't sleep, even after they stopped.'"

I thought for a couple minutes. I saw the daily commute to work, the villages, the children. I understood a little more clearly the fear that must have been in the hearts of the workers. The rebuilding wasn't just another construction process. People were afraid for their lives.

"Tell me more about the stories," I said.

2. Nehemiah 4:12.

Nehemiah leaned forward. "Leaders tell stories that lay out the values, that remind people in the group why the group exists. And they tell these stories over and over, even *in* times of crisis. Maybe even to *prevent* times of crisis.

"You started this conversation as a way to talk about the last half of chapter 8. You wanted to talk about the Feast of Booths as a lived-out story. But I don't think that when you started, you understood the significance of the repetition of stories."

He was right on both counts. I did want to cover some material. And I did get surprised when we started.

"How did you repeat the stories?" I asked.

"First, I told the story of the broken walls to encourage my heart to start, to capture the king's heart, to resist the temptation to quit. Remember how many times I talked about it? 'The city is in ruins, the gates are burned.'[3] That story was the genesis of the project. *As you lead, remind people of the significant problem you are solving together.*

"Second, I told the story of God's work in Susa to encourage the people to start.[4] When I first got to Jerusalem, they didn't know me, though they knew my family. I needed to tell them who I was and what God did. If you hadn't figured it out, chapters 1 and 2 are the summary of what I told them. *As you lead, remind people of God's involvement from the start.*

"Third, I told the story of God's power to strengthen hearts in the middle of the journey.[5] In the middle of every

3. Just a reminder: Nehemiah 1:3, 2:8, 2:13, 2:17.
4. Nehemiah 2:18.

project, people get tired. To fight the gossip and the news, they need the big picture, the real story. *As you lead, remind the people of God's power.*

"Fourth, God gave the feasts as annual stories to build us into a people. After we finished the wall, we started into the cycle of feasts. As we'll see in a moment, the Feast of Booths is a perfect example of how God taught us to remember the story. He gave us symbolic behavior to act out the time in the wilderness. *As you lead, make the lessons visual.*"

I looked up. "We talked about that visual idea with the shaking out the folds of your robe."

"Precisely. People need to see what an invisible God looks like. So God gives feasts and celebrations and ceremonies for us to live out as reminders and explanations and incarnations of his story.

"Let's go back to *Nehemiah*. On the day after the New Year's celebration, the leaders went back to Ezra. They wanted to know more about a feast he had mentioned in his reading. So he unrolled the scroll to the very end of Deuteronomy. On the day that Moses blessed the people and blessed Joshua, he highlighted the importance of the Feast of Booths.

At the end of every seven years, in the year for canceling debts, during the Festival of Tabernacles, when all Israel comes to appear before the Lord your God at the place he will choose, you shall read this law before them in their hear-

5. Nehemiah 4:14

ing. Assemble the people—men, women and children, and the foreigners residing in your towns—so they can listen and learn to fear the Lord your God and follow carefully all the words of this law. Their children, who do not know this law, must hear it and learn to fear the Lord your God as long as you live in the land you are crossing the Jordan to possess.[6]

"Children may not understand the big sermons, the theology textbooks. But picture this.[7] A family goes out into the country and cuts branches from palm trees and poplars. Because this is right after harvest, they also get the best fruit from the trees. They come home and build a little shelter with the branches. It was pretty fragile. They spend the week sleeping in the shelter. They still go about their work, except on the Sabbaths, but their home life revolves around this booth.

"Their kids say, 'why are we doing this?' And the parents say, 'because God took us out of Egypt. And we spent 40 years in the wilderness. During that whole time, God gave us manna. God kept our clothes from wearing out. God protected us.'"

Nehemiah sat back thoughtfully. "Every year we were supposed to build these little booths. It was like an annual camping trip. Every year we were reminded, and our kids were reminded. *As you lead, live out the stories that God gave you to live.*"

---

6. *Deuteronomy 31:10-13.*
7. Check out what Moses said in Leviticus 23:39-43.

We sat for a bit, thinking about kids and stories and learning and living the why of the people.

"That was a pretty big tent party that year," I said. "Biggest since Joshua?"[8]

"We celebrated well," he replied. "We partied like no one had since Joshua held the first celebrations of this feast. Because we knew what it was like to have no story."

And then he was gone.

8. Nehemiah 8:18.

CONFESSING THE STORY

Nehemiah 9

"You are pretty sneaky," I said to Nehemiah. I'd just gotten home from a discussion of his memoir. He was sitting in my extra desk chair, waiting.

"What's the basis of that accusation?" he asked, calmly. I think he knew my comment was more admiration than accusation.

"In our study, we were looking at chapter 9 of your memoir. It's the story about gathering on the twenty-fourth day of the seventh month. I realized that if someone didn't read any of the rest of the Old Testament, any of the rest of the Law and the Prophets, from just this chapter they would learn the story of 'Patient God and the People of Israel.'"

He just smiled.

"In fact, I was talking to a friend about all the repetition in Paul's writing and explained that he was writing to different groups and situations. Each time he needed to write as if this might be the only letter they ever read. You are doing the same thing here. If the only thing that got passed along was this memoir, you wanted to be sure that people got the point."

"Isn't that what you do, too?" he asked.

It was my turn to be quiet. He was exactly right. I have lots of conversations. Sometimes they are with people, sometimes they are in my head. But I believe it matters to take those conversations and distill them and pass them on. I work to understand the basics of belief, the central story, and weave that into everything I do. It's why we're having these conversations. Nehemiah and I. And you and I.

"So tell me about that day in Jerusalem," I said.

"We'd spent time that month celebrating the completion of the wall and the time to breathe a bit. As we said before, the wall wasn't finished, mind you. Not enough for the dedication ceremony which would come later. But the perimeter was set. We could start feeling safe, feeling like a people. And, as you know, we celebrated the Feast of Booths with great passion.

"Now we were ready to take the next step. It's that feeling you have on January 3. The celebration is done. The holidays are over. And you look in the mirror and take stock of where you are and what's next.

"This gathering was that kind of day. For our people, it's the day we begin reading the stories from the beginning, the stories of the beginning. In fact, you now call it *Bereshit*, "In the beginning." We dressed in humble clothes. We spent the first part of the day hearing God's words. And then it was our turn. It was time for confession."

"Who wrote this confession?" I asked. Most of chapter 9 is a confession.

Nehemiah avoided the question. "As you can read, it was the Levites who spoke this to God, on behalf of the people. Leaders can give words to the cry of people's hearts. They can help those hearts cry. And, you will remember, we had just stood through a reading of Deuteronomy."

I decided not to push about authorship of the prayer. "When I read this prayer," I said, "I'm amazed at its scope. It covers millennia, from Creation to Abram to Mount Sinai. And in that first part, every thought starts with 'God'. There's a relentless rhythm. Reading it out loud, you and the rest of the people must have been overwhelmed with God. Reading it off a page loses some of that power."

He nodded. "It *is* oral. You forget sometimes that almost everything was out loud until a millennium after me, even reading. And this prayer is communal. We are hearing this and being moved by this and joining in this confession together."

I understood. "So when the Levites got to the 'But they, our forefathers', it had to be an ominous feeling.'"

"It was. It marks a turning point in the confession. Having acknowledged to God our understanding of all that *he* had done, this 'but' is like a punch in the stomach. And then the Levites reminded us that God did not give up at

1. Nehemiah 9:16.

the first offense. There was forbearance. There was forgiveness. There was a renewal of blessing through the wilderness, through the conquest."

"But isn't this a little too much of a summary? Don't the books of Moses record a lot of disobedience in the lives of the people even before verse 16?"

Nehemiah smiled. "Remember perspective. In the account of the Levites, their goal is to highlight the trends. Where is the story taking people? Yes, there were lots of individual rebellions and restorations, but the trend is that God brought us to this land, and once our forebearers got to this land, we wavered. In the same way that the long history is of God moving across millennia to bring us here, our time here was a constant bickering with each other and with him.

"That's why, if you were to draw this prayer on a flipchart, you would start with a long line going from left to right representing God taking his people to the Promised Land. Then a short line back to the left (rebellion), then a long line going to the right, and then a zigzag scribble and then a line straight down to exile."

I pictured it. It made sense.

"And then at the end of the line?" I said.

"At the end of the line we are turning to God. Carefully, reverently, but hopefully. 'Do not let the hardship seem trifling in your eyes' was as humble as we could be in our request."[2]

I read the end of their confession out loud:

2. Nehemiah 9:32.

But see, we are slaves today, slaves in the land you gave our forefathers so they could eat its fruit and the other good things it produces. Because of our sins, its abundant harvest goes to the kings you have placed over us. They rule over our bodies and our cattle as they please. We are in great distress.[3]

"There's poignancy to the ending of this prayer. You are saying to God, 'and after all this, we're back in the Promised Land, with these walls. But there's still a foreign king. We're still in bondage. We need you.'"

"Isn't that always the prayer of God's people?" he said. "We're never quite home even when it seems like home? Aren't we always standing before God, confessing our inadequacies, our personal and generational sins, our need of him?"

"This confession is where you started when you first heard of the ruins, isn't it?" I asked.

He smiled. "Now you are beginning to understand. The broken walls were real, but they also stood for our brokenness. And when I prayed for God to restore us, I wanted the walls to be restored. But I understood that God wanted the people to be restored as well. He didn't want a city, he wanted a community of faithful people."

Nehemiah walked out.

And I tried to summarize:

The book of Nehemiah constantly tells the stories of redemption, rejection, repentance, and renewal. God redeems us. We

---

3. *Nehemiah 9:36-37.*

reject God. We repent of our rejection. God renews his promises. And the cycle starts. Chapter 9 reviews it clearly so that if all someone reads is just this one book, they get the story of a man who followed God, and they get the story of a people who didn't.

THE SIX ROUTINES

Nehemiah 10

I wanted to empty my inbox before the weekend. I opened an email from a friend. I knew I wasn't going to meet my goal.

The message was a description of a difficult situation, a betrayal in a relationship. I knew both parties. I didn't want to take sides. But it was clear that one side was the offender, one side was the violator, one side had acted with flagrant disregard for the other. I needed to provide some counsel.

I looked over my shoulder at Nehemiah. He was sitting quietly, sipping coffee. His right finger was tracing some letters, but it just looked like "w o y".[1] Nothing I recognized. I tilted my chair slightly, making it squeak.

"What comes after 'I'm sorry'?" I said as Nehemiah looked up.

"What do you mean?" he asked.

1. Of course, in English it meant nothing. In Hebrew it was probably *sh'ma*. I just didn't know Hebrew well enough. And Nehemiah was simply praying, even with his finger.

"All the time we get into trouble. All the time we do foolish things that we don't mean and wrong things that we mean. All the time we hurt people, break relationships, fall short of our intentions. And then we stop the bad behavior. We say, 'I'm sorry'. But that doesn't seem like enough."

Nehemiah was blunt. "It's not."

That didn't help. "I know," I said. 'We feel a need to make up for our offenses, somehow. But some offenses can't be mended. A betrayal can't be un-betrayed. Years of rejection can't be restored. A slandered reputation seems stained forever."

Nehemiah actually looked sympathetic. "Time cannot be replaced," he said quietly. "But the relationship may be restored."

I looked confused.

Nehemiah smiled. "I think that you have a more complete understanding of reconciliation than we had. God's told you more of his story than he had told us. But I can tell you what that step after 'I'm sorry' looked like for us. And then you can decide what to tell your friends.

"You and I already talked about the confession we made. We acknowledged who God was and what he had asked us to do. We clearly identified what we had done wrong. We acknowledge that it was wrong. We asked for favor from God.

"At that point, 'I'm sorry' was as much as we could do about the immediate problem–it stopped our headlong run away from someone and started a conversation with them. But stopping is only part of the process. It doesn't change the direction we are moving. We have to turn around and start living a different way.

"In the case of your friends, there may have been vows that they took about the way they were going to live their lives. In our case, we had a clear set of directions from God about how to live. We acknowledged that we hadn't been living that way. The next obvious step was to start living that way again."

I held up my hand. "May I interrupt for a minute. You skipped the list of names that comes right after your group confession."

Nehemiah shook his head. "I'm talking about restoring relationship with God and you are asking about a list of names?"

"But aren't you the one who taught me about the importance of names?" It had been several weeks since we talked about the list of people who rebuilt the wall, but I had to believe that this list was an important part of the confession and repentance.

Nehemiah was quiet for a few minutes. When he started, it was clear that I hadn't been reading closely enough. "The list of names, what you call Nehemiah 10:1-27, isn't part of the confession and repentance text. It's like a footnote to explain the end of what you call Nehemiah 9:38. The document itself, the written-out prayer to God, reads

In view of all this, we are making a binding agreement, putting it in writing, and our leaders, our Levites and our priests are affixing their seals to it....The rest of the peo-

*ple—priests, Levites, gatekeepers, musicians, temple servants
and all who separated themselves from the neighboring peoples for the sake of the Law of God, together with their wives
and all their sons and daughters who are able to understand— all these now join their fellow Israelites the nobles...*

"Since you stopped me, yes, the names are important. But
at this point, what's more important than each of the names
is that we were simply saying that in this confession and
recommitment, we were all together. From the youngest
child to the governor, we were the people of God."

I held out my hands in apology. "I was wanting to show
off," I said. "I do that. I'm sorry. Would you start again?"

Nehemiah smiled. "Exactly right," he said. And then
laughed at the confusion on my face. "Although it seems too
simple, when we approached God we said, 'we're sorry. May
we start again.' And the commitments that follow are our
understanding of what starting again looks like."

It made sense. A little. "And then you approached God.
You took a curse and an oath. Was it like 'cross my heart and
hope to die?'"

"Remember Moses and Solomon?" Nehemiah said. "We
talked about them when we talked about my prayer.
Solomon had described what would happen if we obeyed
and what would happen if we didn't. There was blessing and
curse there. We were simply accepting those terms again
now that we were back in Jerusalem from the ends of the
earth. After all we'd been through, we didn't worry about

the curse part. There was no way that we would turn from God. That's what we believed.

"What we were focusing on was the future, returning to the path that God had laid out. We were simply promising to obey God's law. That was the oath.

"The Law was what had been given to Moses. Commands, ordinances, and statutes, we were going to do it all. And we were going to do whatever we could to extend the obedience to the next generation. We were limiting the local influences. Who our kids married mattered. We were rebuilding a people, and a people need a purpose and boundaries."

I thought for a bit. "It seems harsh," I said. "All these limits on marriage and acceptance of rules. It seems restrictive until it makes sense. I mean, we all do it. We all are concerned about our group identity. And when we are trying to mend a relationship, it makes sense to consider the likes and dislikes of the person you wronged."

Nehemiah nodded. "We had contact with others. I was working in the court of a conquering kingdom, after all. But what is the nature of that contact? We talk with them, we buy from them. But there needed to be constraints, the things that identified us as us. The rule breathes."

"Really? When I read through the list of things that you were agreeing to do, they seem to cover all of life. Wasn't it restrictive?"

Nehemiah smiled. "It's time for us to talk about routine. Sometimes restriction sounds like a bad thing. And sometimes it is. But when we are thinking about a way of living, following God's way, it's possible that there are restrictions that make sense."

I started thinking about the idea of routine: a set of thoughts and behaviors performed consistently. What if there were routines that were healthy and helpful.

Nehemiah interrupted my thoughts.

"Number your paper from 1 to 6." he said.

I groaned.

Nehemiah smiled. "You see how that simple action puts you in a learning mode?"

"It puts me in a testing mode," I said. "It reminds me of all the quizzes in school that I wasn't ready for."

"Exactly," he said. "Actions can remind us of the context where we used that action before. In this case, for you, the context of quizzes is an unpleasant reminder of your own unwise behavior. But what if you had actually studied when you were in school? In that case, the process of numbering your paper would have reminded you of the times when you got to show to yourself and your teacher that you had learned something, right?"

As much as I disliked the reminder of my poor study habits, I understood. Repeated actions shape us and can then remind us of the context. It can be a bad thing, like flashbacks, or it can be a very helpful thing, like being reminded of commitments.

"Back to the list. I know that sometime you are planning to talk about how I was shaped by reading the Law. This will be an illustration. I want to give you six kinds of routines that God put in place to remind us regularly about his work.

They are all folded together in our promises to God in chapter 10, but I want to lay them out more simply.

"*First, there were daily routines.* You remember how I had talked to God morning and evening for four months as I was wondering how the walls could be rebuilt? That morning and evening prayer had been part of my routine long before my brother came with the bad news. Morning and evening prayer was part of our story as a people. The Levites prayed in front of the altar morning and evening.[2] David had prayers, psalms, for morning and evening.[3] Through Moses, God laid out morning and evening sacrifices.[4] He said there was to be an offering all the time, but he specified morning and evening to start the offerings. When you are offering a lamb, it takes that long."

I interrupted, "But we're not doing burnt offerings any more. And no one has, Jew or Christian, since the temple was destroyed in 70 AD."

I was relieved by that, since I'm not a fan of blood.

He paused. "Do you think that the removal of the sacrifice means that you don't need daily reminders?"

He was right. Paul talked about making ourselves living sacrifices.[5] Maybe looking at the *when* of the sacrifice rather than the what might teach me about routine. And maybe,

---

2. David outlined their duties in 1 Chronicles 23, and specified their daily prayer routine: "They were also to stand every morning to thank and praise the Lord. They were to do the same in the evening and whenever burnt offerings were presented to the Lord on the Sabbaths, at the New Moon feasts and at the appointed festivals" (1 Chronicles 23:30-31).
3. Psalm 4 is an evening prayer, for example.
4. In Numbers 28.
5. Romans 12:1.

when Jesus talked about daily bread, he was creating a daily routine.

"Let's go back to the list please?" Nehemiah's quiet voice broke in.

"*Second, there were weekly routines.* I'm sure you have noticed that Sabbath was a big deal for me. I made a point out of closing the gates for Sabbath."[6]

"I've wanted to talk to you about that. Why so much about gates?" I asked.

"That's for later. For now, Sabbath. It was a weekly reminder of God's rest after creation and God's rescue of his people from Egypt. We can pause daily, but we need a longer time each week to refresh and remember. To set aside our lists and remember that the strength and direction come from God."

I sensed that he had much more to say about this subject. I do, too. But not here, not today.

"*Third, there were monthly reminders.* You've heard that leaders should reinforce vision every 28 days or so? That's every four weeks. That's why God told the people to make a sacrifice every new moon."

"But don't the prophets talk about God not liking their New Moon celebrations?"

"Ah, you've been searching Biblegateway.com for 'new moon', haven't you. It's easy to turn a routine, a way of living, into a ritual. We perform a ritual, hoping it has some

---

6. Nehemiah 13:15-22.

value in itself. It's a kind of magic. You wear your lucky underwear. You show up to church every week.

"And God said, through his prophets, that we as a people had started doing these rituals to placate him, or without thinking. Our bodies did the sacrifice, our minds were somewhere else. Sometime read the way Malachi reams out the priests.[7] But just because we ritualize behavior doesn't mean that we shouldn't look at routine.

"Think of it this way: a ritual is something we do hoping to influence God. A routine is something we do to work on us. A routine like daily prayer or weekly Sabbath or monthly celebration brings our minds back to the story of God's work. But thinking about a routine this way means we have to think about what we are doing rather than ritually acting."

"I'm not sure I understand."

"I know," Nehemiah said. "That's why we keep having these conversations. As we *routinely* look at the text, at the stories, at the works of God, we keep getting glimpses that we wouldn't otherwise have if we didn't routinely talk." He smiled. "If you want a practical application of the 28 days thinking, go back to the wall rebuilding. Halfway through the project everyone was getting discouraged. We made

---

7. For example, in Malachi 2: "And now, you priests, this warning is for you. If you do not listen, and if you do not resolve to honor my name," says the Lord Almighty, "I will send a curse on you, and I will curse your blessings. Yes, I have already cursed them, because you have not resolved to honor me. Because of you I will rebuke your descendants; I will smear on your faces the dung from your festival sacrifices, and you will be carried off with it."

some changes, reviewed our purpose, looked again to God's presence. We needed to get refocused."

I hadn't thought about the wall story that way. I looked at the cycles of attention in my life. I wondered how often I ran out of steam after a month or so. I made a note to look at the calendar for the moon schedule.

"*Fourth, there were annual reminders.* We talked a couple weeks ago about the festival occasions for storytelling. In the course of a year, we covered all the stories of God's work. They came with reminders of our failures or struggles. The focus wasn't on our failure, but on God's mighty hand and outstretched arm."

I raised my hand. "You mean like spending time at New Year's looking back at the year and looking ahead?"

He smiled. "Exactly. And at Advent. And Lent. And Easter. And Pentecost. All those times that you could use to understand God's work. Instead you complain about the holidays that Hallmark has created. But think about it. People need celebrations and reminders. Hallmark is just meeting a need for reflection.

"We're running out of time but I want to cover these last two. *Fifth, there were reminders every seven years.* God had laid out a Sabbath year, a time when debts were cancelled and the land wasn't worked and we were supposed to remember that God had given us a Promised Land. The land was created by God, given by God, watered by God."

"Wasn't the exile related to this?"

Nehemiah looked down. "The exile and slavery lasted until the kingdom of Persia took over. This is exactly the message of God that Jeremiah had preached. The land was made desolate, put to an extended Sabbath rest, a seventy-year Sabbath rest making up for all the unkept Sabbaths." He was quoting from 2 Chronicles 36.[8]

"*Sixth, there were once in a lifetime celebrations.* The dedication of the wall was one of these. The biggest one God described the year of Jubilee, every fifty years. It was a sabbath of Sabbath years. It was supposed to be huge. I'm not sure we ever did it.

"But I tried to help us celebrate these ways. I spent the rest of my life routinely reminding our people of the stories of God."

"Wasn't that how you ended your account of your life?"

He walked away. "I'm not ready for that conversation yet," he said.

I understood. "But what about my friends," I said.

"I'm not sure what to tell you," he said. "You have to sort out the best way to offer counsel. You have to decide whether they are ready for reconciliation. But for me, calling people to return to God's way, to follow confession and repentance with a return to the routines God laid out for us, makes sense. We can't make up for bad living, but we can live right from now on."

---

8. But Nehemiah could have gone even further back. In Leviticus 26:33-39 God warns that there will be exile so the land can have its rest.

IN WHICH WE TALK ABOUT THE LISTS OF NAMES

Nehemiah 3, 7, 8, 10, 11, 12

I was sitting in a college coffee shop, waiting for Hope to get out of class. It was a dad-daughter date of sorts. And I had an hour on my own.

I paged through my mind, looking at projects. Nehemiah 10 was written on the top of one page, the next place we needed to go in this discussion. I thought through the chapter. I opened my eyes. Nehemiah sat on the tall chair across from me where my backpack had been.

I looked at Nehemiah. "Again with the names," I whispered. "How many times do you have to list all these names? What are we supposed to do with them? How much time am I supposed to spend reflecting on their significance?"

We had talked before about the great review of history

that the Levites did. We had talked about the commitments that the people made. And right between those two lofty and convicting discussions is a list of the people who signed the commitment.

"Don't you sign important documents anymore?" Nehemiah asked. "When your elders published a vision statement for your church a few years ago, didn't you all make a big deal out of signing with of your names? When there was that Declaration of Independence, didn't people sign it? And don't you tell stories about what it cost them to sign?

"Names matter. Your name matters to you. The commitments you make with your name matter to you. And when your story is told, doesn't your name matter?"

I nodded. "But it feels like half this book is names. I understand your point, but when I read the Bible I want to know how to apply what I read, and I don't know what to do with the names."

Nehemiah smiled. He looked around at the students sitting in the coffee shop. "You are a little surprised, right now. You thought this was a story about a great work. You thought we were going to be talking about leadership or management. And I'm going to ask you to do a Bible study, just like the other learners in this room. It will be good for you.

"In that notebook, make a list of the lists of names and their locations in this book. It will be tedious. But by the end, I think you'll understand."

I didn't grumble too much. But I did feel like I was back in college. I wrote out a list in my notebook.

- *The people who built the wall. Nehemiah 3.*
- *A list of the tribes and families who returned to Jerusalem in the first wave a century before Nehemiah. Nehemiah 7:4-69. (I didn't ask who counted the donkeys.)*
- *A list of the leaders and Levites who stood with Ezra and translated for Ezra. Nehemiah 8.*
- *The leaders, Levites and priests who signed the document. Nehemiah 10:1-27.*
- *The people (1 in 10) who settled in Jerusalem. Nehemiah 11.*
- *The priests and Levites who came in the first wave and some subsequent generations. Nehemiah 12 . (I realized this was some of the detail of the chapter 7 list, but without the donkeys.)*
- *The leaders, priests and Levites who led the dedication of the wall. Nehemiah 12:27-47.*

"Very good," Nehemiah said. "So, tell me what you see in those lists."

"You list people who do the hard work, who take the big risks."

"Good," he said. "The building teams, the Jerusalem residents, the leaders signing on the dotted line, the first returners. It's important to acknowledge their sacrifice. What else?"

"You list the people who have to take responsibility.

Like the leaders in Chapter 11 who say that they are going to obey."

"Exactly. There is an accountability factor that comes from publishing the names of the people who make promises. What else?"

I began to understand what the people I teach feel like when I keep pushing. "You list the lineage of the religious leaders."

"Good. The priests and Levites must have a clear connection back to Aaron and Levi. We kept close track of these connections. Regularly recording these genealogies meant that the people could be sure that those who were teaching the Law were living in the tradition of the Law."

I looked up at him. "Why does this matter so much to you? As I think about it, I realize that we don't know your lineage. We know your dad's name, and that's it.[1] You weren't a Levite, were you?"

I didn't want to sound accusatory. But he took some time to answer.

"I'm not sure that's for you to know. What does matter is that regardless of my lineage, I did everything I could to honor God and his leaders and his worship and his people."

We sat and drank coffee. It was cold. But it filled the silence between us. I changed the subject a little.

"I understand the lists a bit better, but I think that part of my question about how to understand them relates to the

---

1. It was Hakaliah. Nehemiah 1:1.

choppiness of the text. The story feels interrupted by the lists."

It was his turn to push me a little.

"Think about that dark green filing cabinet in your office. The one with all the projects you haven't finished? Picture the genealogy folder. Think about what's in it. There are a couple of family trees from your Uncle Gordie. There's a family history from some distant cousin. There are a couple letters from your mom. There are photocopies of obituaries.

"When you get around to writing a family history for your kids, the first draft will look like all of those pieces spread out on this table, with introductory comments written on Post-It notes, and hand-written pages of some of the other stories. The second draft will look like a series of typed pages. But anyone reading it will benefit from remembering that this part is from you, that part is from your uncle, the other part is from an obituary. A wise reader will read it as a collection of historical documents, not a novel where the story can be fabricated to make the story flow."

"So you are suggesting that the choppiness is part of the historicity of the text?"

"I am. And so are all the names. You find lots of confusing lists of names in historical documents. You don't find as much lineage in mythology."

"Except for Tolkien." I said. "He just loved the words and names."

Nehemiah looked blank.

JON SWANSON

"Never mind. So this isn't a management conversation, this is a 'how the Bible came to be' conversation?"

"Why does it have to be either/or? Can't you do both in the same writing? Your daughter is coming. Let's finish up. Here are your lessons.

1. The **records** matter. That's why we kept them.
2. The **threads of history** matter. That's why we trace people and families and tribes through generations.
3. The **people** matter. Each name on each list is a person, created and loved by God. Like me. Like you.
4. The **people's interaction with geography** matters. Real people built the wall. Real people marched on the wall. Real people stood in front of the wall and explained what God said and Ezra read."

As I finished writing down his words, Hope walked up. "Hi Daddy," she said. "I hope I didn't keep you waiting."

I turned to introduce her to Nehemiah. But all we saw was a backpack on a chair.

And two empty cups.

"You drank mine, too?" she said.

IN WHICH WE TALK ABOUT KEEPING FOCUS

Nehemiah's Life

I looked over at Nehemiah. "Did you ever lose focus?"

He looked up. He had been resting. Or praying. I never can tell. "What do you mean?"

I sounded desperate as I rushed through my explanation. "I mean, did you ever get distracted from your work, start too many things, get into the middle of something and not know how to finish it?"

Nehemiah thought for a moment, letting my question hang in the air between us. "What do you think?" he said, finally.

"Well, it looks like *you* did an amazing job of staying on task, of persisting," I said. I tried not to whine. But I wasn't doing a very good job. I was feeling the press of too many promises.

He smiled. "You are only seeing the highlights, the turning points. Why do you think I'm any less human that you are? Any less prone to distraction? Just because I was living before the kinds of technology you have, doesn't mean there weren't things that got in the way, other subjects to think about, other scrolls to read. All those times where you read that I responded, that I took time before answering, do you think I was *born* with that kind of discipline?"

"Of course not," I answered, not exactly convinced.

"What you are reading is a God-guided case study of how we built the wall first and then the nation. What you are reading leaves out all the parts about my momentary doubts, my hesitation before plunging in. Because those aren't nearly as important to the whole story as the habits that were formed, the discipline that developed over years.

"Let me give you a quick list of habits. Maybe we'll expand them later, maybe you'll figure them out."

I sat back, fingers on the keyboard. I needed some structure right now.

"**First, I tried to get my priorities from God.** We've talked about this before. I find that if I know that the project or the work or the day is consistent with God's priorities, that self-discipline is easier. Not in a guilty way, but in a clarifying way. If there are six projects in front of me and one is consistent with God's way of talking and writing and teaching, then the decision about what to do next is much clearer. If two of the six are, it's a little harder, but I can get rid of four choices. For me, when the king said 'what's bothering you?' I knew that it was time to commit. When we were dealing with all the attacks from Sanballat and Tobiah, I knew that it was my job to lead and protect."

I stopped him. "But when do you know when to go? When is it clear that it's time to move?" I was thinking about all the times that I couldn't decide what God wanted.

Nehemiah hesitated. "I know this is a big deal for you. But I'm not sure exactly what to tell you. Maybe I needed to just keep explaining. Because **second, and very related, I talked with God.**

I talked with God all the time. Four months at the beginning. When I talked to the king. When we were facing attacks. Even at the end of the story, when we list several last challenges, I included my prayer just to show you the kinds of things we talked about. I know that it sounds like bragging, but I was just being honest with you readers about how honest I was with God. There were lots of times I didn't talk to God. But I made sure that there were several of my short prayers included in the book. I didn't want anyone to think that I was a great leader just on my own."

He stopped, suddenly emotional. I tried to help him out.

I said, "You know, just this week I saw a video from another pastor, Bill Hybels.[1] He talked about a guy who had morning coffee with God. He picked a rocking chair, turned it toward a nice view, had a place to put his coffee cup, got up 15 minutes earlier, and talked with God. Hybels told

---

1. Bill Hybels. "Coffee with God." Online video clip. *YouTube*. YouTube, 4 August 2010. http://www.youtube.com/watch?v=-xU9GR4H0WQ. Accessed 11/2/13.

about two decades of hearing the man describe the results of those conversations. That sounds like you. We just read some of the results, forgetting that you and God had talked a lot."

Nehemiah had recovered. "Thanks. That's a great transition to the next habit. **Third, I kept the routines.**

"One thing I mention in my memoir is that one of the final things I did was to make sure the wood was being provided for the fire on the altar. It's not exciting, but filling the woodbox day after day so the sacrifices could happen day after day is a spiritual act. And the pure physicality of it kept me focused. If you read carefully, you will see that keeping the Sabbath was something that mattered to me. Mostly because it mattered to God.

"Every day, fire. Every week, Sabbath. Every year, the appropriate feasts. Every morning..."

"...every morning, coffee," I finished. "With God."

"Right," he said. And took a sip. "Moving on. **Fourth, I reviewed the stories.** When I first met with the people in Jerusalem to talk about starting the wall, I told them everything that had gotten me to this point. Reviewing the stories mattered. My first prayer reviewed the story of God's relationship. In chapter 9, we reviewed that story in detail.

"If you get stuck and are wondering why something matters, I think reviewing the stories of how you got here and what God's doing might help."

I thought for a minute. "So let me review. Follow God, talk to God, do the routines, review the stories. That sounds good, but it sounds pretty basic, pretty ... routine. What did other people think about how simple you were?"

Nehemiah smiled at me, as if he had been waiting for that question. "You are going to hate this one. **Fifth, I didn't get nearly as sidetracked as you do, worrying about what people were going to think.**"

I thought once again how annoying it is that he can read my mind. As if he lived in my head.

"My focus was on doing what God said," he said. "But I see I don't need to explain that one so let's keep going. Which is the next habit. **Sixth, I just kept going.** If you read all the way through, you see that there were lots of times that stuff wasn't working. But I didn't ever worry about it being my fault, thinking that I should quit the project. I tried not to be arrogant. I listened to what the people were saying and responded and didn't get upset. But I was confident that God was working somehow, and that the single most important thing I could do was to push on, to keep building, to keep obeying.

"Now, don't forget that I didn't go too far. While the wall was the project, I worked on the wall. I didn't build armies. I didn't go out to attack. I didn't let us get distracted. We just built the wall. Later, I focused on helping the people rebuild their lives. We focused on the temple, the giving, the worship, the obedience to God.

"We were in this whole mess because we didn't follow God's Law, because we didn't keep Sabbath. I wasn't going to let that happen as long as I had influence."

He paused. I said, "This is great. But this is a lot."

He smiled. "If this is all too complicated, my friend Ezra made a really simple commitment. He was committed to learning the Law, observing the Law and teaching the Law.[2] It wasn't easy, but never confuse *simple* with *easy*. Sometimes the simplest next step is incredibly hard."

He stood up. "I need to go. But here's something to think about when you are worrying about focus.

"Relax a little. Don't get so wrapped up in being perfect, in getting everything exactly right. We built the wall poorly, but we got it done. Because the wall was the most important thing. Just keep learning to do the most important thing. Sometimes you learn it by trying two or three things and discover that God doesn't care about which of those things you choose. He cares about you."

And he was gone.

I settled down. I started writing.

"I looked over at Nehemiah. 'Did you ever lose focus?'" I typed.

2. Ezra 7:10.

IN WHICH WE TALK ABOUT KEEPING PROMISES

Nehemiah 13

"Hi," I said to Nehemiah. "It's been awhile."

"I'm always here," he said.

I smiled at him. "I know. I'm grateful. Were you worried that I wouldn't follow through on my promise a couple weeks ago?" I had taken some time away from our weekly conversations. I had said that I would be back, but we humans often struggle with doing what we know we ought to do.

"No, I knew you'd be back. But I also knew that the sooner we started our conversations again, the better. When we take a break from our routines, there is always a risk that we won't start again."

"You are talking about what happened after the people made all their promises in chapter 10, aren't you."

He nodded.

"Do you mind if we connect those promises to what happened in Chapter 13?"

"No," he said. "As long as you aren't trying to hurry me out of your life."

"That will never happen," I said.

"That's exactly what the people promised," he said. "They made vows and invited a curse. But vows and curses run into how people are."

"We call that human nature," I said.

"Whatever. I call it frustrating and I call it the reality of leadership."

"Do you mind if I try to summarize what happened? And then you can correct me?"

Nehemiah sat back. "Go ahead."

"I want to start back at the reading of the Law in chapter 8. Ezra reads, the people feel convicted of their bad behavior, and the Levites lead in a time of confession and commitment. Starting in Chapter 9, they review the history of God's involvement with his people. At the beginning of Chapter 10, a group of political and spiritual leaders sign a document that promises they will return to obedience.

"The document specifies the actions that will be taken. It's the kind of declaration that is still made by gatherings of God's people. There is a confessional component and a covenant component."

"It's what I did in my prayer," Nehemiah said. "Way back in chapter 1."

"Exactly." I replied. "So everyone made these promises in chapter 10. If I can simplify them, there were three: to marry within the faith, to give regularly, and to preserve the Sabbath."

"That's good," Nehemiah said. "There was much more detail in those promises, about how much to give to whom, but that's a good overview. We summarized them at the end by promising 'we will not neglect the house of our God.'"[1]

I went on. "It was an appropriate summary of everything that had happened up to that time in history. You and your colleagues and contemporaries were saying, in essence, 'We know our forefathers messed up. But starting today, we're making a new commitment, a fresh start with God. We're not going to fall into the same traps that ruined previous generations and caused all our problems.'"

Nehemiah nodded. "That's exactly what we were doing. After all I had been through, after all the work and prayer, after Ezra's work and the Levites' work, we were together in this solemn assembly. It was an exciting and humbling moment."

"And then time goes by."

"Right," Nehemiah whispered.

"During the next few years, the people settled back into daily life. Many people settled into the villages around

---

1. Nehemiah 10:39.

Jerusalem. A select few stayed. There was a big dedication of the walls. And then you went back to Susa."

He shrugged. "After 12 years, it was time to go back and report in with the king."

"Was that really your first time back? In that conversation with the King where you laid out your plan, did you tell him that you would be gone for 12 years, and he let you go?"

He smiled at me. "You know that's not important. If it were, we would have recorded it. And don't ask me how long I was gone, either."

"All of us guess that it was awhile. Long enough for Malachi to speak about some of the things that concerned you."[2]

He just looked at me. He knew I was fishing for details.

"Okay. Never mind. So when you came back, whenever that was, things had gotten out of control. There were problems with marriages. There were problems with the offerings. There were problems with the Sabbath. The key things you identified had blown up. It really frustrated you, didn't it? I mean, you pulled out guys' hair."

Nehemiah held up his hand. "I know I said we could talk about this, but can we go into those details later? Or not at all?"

"Okay. But give me a summary of guidelines for keeping spiritual promises."

2. In his commentary on Malachi, Robert Alden says there are two main positions on the timing of Malachi. His prophecy could fall between Ezra and Nehemiah. Or it could come while Nehemiah is back in Susa. See Robert Alden, "Malachi." Vol 7. Pp. 701-725 in *The Expositor's Bible Commentary*. Edited by F. E. Gaebelein. Grand Rapids: Zondervan, p 703.

He thought for a bit. "Let's try these:

1. **When you make promises, make them about the things that matter.** At least that way, when people wander, they are wandering from what is important, and when you call them to repentance, it's a call that is a call back to God.

2. **When you are a leader, remind people of the promises that they made.** Our job is to keep people focused on what we all committed to. It's why we have been called by people and by God. More than anything else, calling people to faithfulness matters.

3. **When you are a servant, you have to follow God, no matter what.** I left Jerusalem and things slowly fell apart. I could have said, 'God, if you had left me here I would have kept them from disobeying.' But that would have been giving myself too much credit.

4. **People struggle to obey.** That's how it is."

He stood up. "You are lucky," he said. "You have the Holy Spirit to keep reminding you of what God wants and means. I bet you never have people getting off track."[3]

It was my turn to just look at him.

His eyes widened.

---

3. Nehemiah was pointing to a conversation Jesus had with his disciples. The Holy Spirit would come, Jesus said, and would "teach you all things and remind you of everything I have said to you" (John 14:29). From Nehemiah's perspective, this kind of consistent divine prompting would have been welcome during the time he was away from the people.

"You mean God's people aren't all perfect now?"

IN WHICH WE TALK ABOUT NEHEMIAH'S RETURN

Nehemiah 12:12-13:9

I was reading Nehemiah 12:12-13:9.

"What day was it, exactly?" I said. I turned to Nehemiah, waiting for an answer.

He waited.

"You led a huge celebration of the completion of the wall. The celebration finishes.

"We read, 'at that time men were appointed to be in charge of the storerooms.'¹And then we read about the whole history of priests and Levites, singers and gatekeepers.

"And then we read, 'On that day the Book of Moses was

---

1. Nehemiah 12:44.

read aloud.'² And then we read about the Ammonites and the Moabites.

"And then we read 'Before this, Eliashib the priest had been put in charge of the storerooms.'³ And we read about Tobiah living in the temple.

"And then we read 'But while all this was going on, I was not in Jerusalem.'⁴

"And then we read about what you did with Tobiah when you got back and about the Levites not getting the offerings and going back to their towns. So, pick any of those things. What day was it, exactly?"

He took a sip of his coffee. He looked out the window. The snow was mostly gone. The squirrels were able to eat acorns. For several weeks, they had been limited to a diet of birdseed tossed from the birdfeeders by active juncos.

"Why do you want to know?" he said.

I was not expecting that question.

I paused. Then I said, "Because I want to tell the story, your story. A storyteller needs to know the narrative structure, to have a flow of the story. It makes no sense right now. 'At that time', 'the same day', 'before that', 'but I wasn't there'. That's crazy talk. That's why people have questions about the Bible. 'Why should I believe this? It's so confusing. It's contradictory.'"

"But why do you want to know?" he asked again. "Are you doubting?"

2. Nehemiah 13:1-3.
3. Nehemiah 13:4.
4. Nehemiah 13:6.

"No," I said. "Not at all. But I like to be able to explain."

He leaned forward. "Think about it this way. What if you could see the lines in the original text that we've talked about before, the Post-It notes and hand-scrawled notes? What if you looked at the lines that are there?"

"What lines?"

"Okay. There's the story about the dedication of the walls. It ends with a summary about the amount of noise. Then there's another section, this time talking very clearly about the care of the offerings and the temple workers. Then there's another section, about reading the book of Moses."

I slapped my head.

"What is it?"

"You just have to actually stop and read the text, don't you?"

"What?"

"I finally get it, at least part of my confusion. Chapter 13 is backwards."

"What?"

"I know that you were just writing sentences, not chapters. But at the beginning of what we call chapter 13 we read, 'On that day.' And I asked, 'What day?' Because I thought that 'on that day' was talking about the day the dedication happened. But now that I'm actually stopping and reading this, here's what I think:

"This is written like I write sometimes, or better, like I talk. The first few sentences, the sentences about reading the book of Moses and talking about the Moabites, if we were to put those words on a timeline, they come after you kicked Tobiah out."

Nehemiah smiled at my enthusiasm. "I know what you mean, but I think you better explain for the readers at home."

"Okay. Let me try telling the story.

"In the days following the dedication of the walls, 'at that time,' people are put in charge of the storerooms in the temple. Facility managers, or administrators, or money guards, or all three. One of them is a priest named Eliashib. We don't know any other names.

"These people had great responsibility. They took offerings people brought and put them in storerooms. Then they distributed them regularly to the priests and Levites.

"Before there was a temple, in the tabernacle days, the Levites carried the tent poles and the awnings and the furniture as the people moved around the wilderness. After things settled down, David appointed some of them to be singers and appointed Asaph to lead the choir and write music. It looked a lot like a church staff today."

He smiled at me. "Spoken like a true executive pastor," he said.

"Eventually, you leave for Susa. It's been twelve years since you came. You have rebuilt the wall. You've been around for a few cycles of the routine. You need to check in with the king.

"You leave someone in charge as governor, perhaps your brother, and you are gone. You neglect to tell us how long. But during that time Eliashib is approached by Tobiah. He was your nemesis from Chapter 2. Eliashib and Tobiah are related somehow. And somehow, Tobiah ends up with a room, an apartment, on the temple campus. Right so far?"

Nehemiah just looked at me.

"When you return, you are stunned, then furious. You toss Tobiah's stuff out of the temple. You clean the room. and you go looking for the storage containers and the offerings. You find some, but you realize that there are fewer Levites around than there should be.

"What you do about that situation will be another story. But that 'same day', when people are wondering what the noise is, you have someone read the book of Moses. the part that talks about what the Moabites and Ammonites did to Israel. The words that are written at the beginning of chapter 13, but happen after verse 9."

Nehemiah smiled. "But why do you want to know?"

I made a list for him:

- "Because it's a powerful story.
- People are appointed as leaders, but they aren't always perfect. They come with baggage. That baggage, left unaddressed, can wreck them.
- Leaders doing dumb stuff with God's stuff isn't new. And it doesn't mean God doesn't exist, it means that we have to clean house.
- Unless we keep renewing our commitments and remembering what God says, we can drift.
- Leaders like you are human. You had to leave. You got to come back and follow up.
- Just because I don't understand the story doesn't

mean I'm dumb or that it's wrong. Sometimes the text takes time."

I looked out the window. "Now, tell me about Tobiah," I said.

When I turned around, he was gone.

IN WHICH WE FINALLY TALK ABOUT TOBIAH

Nehemiah, Deuteronomy, Numbers

Nehemiah and I had been having these conversations for long enough, I thought, that I could risk asking a question I'd been wondering about since chapter 2 of his memoir.

"Tell me about Tobiah," I said to Nehemiah.

He sat silently for a long time. "You know he's a painful person," he replied. It was a statement, not a question. "But it's a fair question. Tobiah was a very difficult opponent during my whole time in Jerusalem. But his story should show you something about God's kind of patience."

I was intrigued with his response. Because I knew that Tobiah had been the single biggest opponent Nehemiah had faced. His influence lasted the whole time Nehemiah was involved with his great work in Jerusalem. Of the three opponents–Sanballat, Tobiah and Geshem–Tobiah was the worst.

"I don't know if I'd say 'worst'," Nehemiah commented. "However, he was the most persistent, most subtle, most politically astute, most connected. And he has a long family story.

"I first met Tobiah soon after we started the project. It was the day I met with the elders, the day after my late-night ride along the walls. The elders and the people had gathered, and I told them about the great work. I told them about all God had done to get me to Jerusalem. It was exhilarating.

"And then, as often happens when a project is just starting, the opposition showed up. We've talked before about the simplicity of my answer.'"

I interrupted. "But I have wondered about what you said. There was a precision about your comment: 'you have no portion or right or claim in Jerusalem.'" [2]

"Ah yes," Nehemiah said. "That statement was pretty absolute, wasn't it? I was actually quoting Moses. In his last message to the people in Deuteronomy, Moses said,

'No Ammonite or Moabite or any of his descendants may enter the assembly of the Lord, even down to the tenth generation. For they did not come to meet you with bread and water on your way when you came out of Egypt, and they hired Balaam son of Beor from Pethor in Aram Naharaim

1. See Chapter 4 of this book: "Facing the resistance of enemies."
2. Nehemiah 2:20 (ESV)

to pronounce a curse on you. However, the Lord your God would not listen to Balaam but turned the curse into a blessing for you, because the Lord your God loves you. Do not seek a treaty of friendship with them as long as you live.' [3]

Nehemiah looked up from the scroll. "The mandate from Moses seemed pretty clear to me. Tobiah's people were to be excluded. And I just wanted Tobiah to know that I knew the old stories."

"That didn't warn him off," I said. "He's around for the rest of the book. But there seems to be a bigger story here than I realized. Can you help me understand?"

Nehemiah leaned back, ready to teach.

"This is a long story, but I'll try to give you the highlights. The story starts with Lot, back in Genesis. Lot was Abraham's nephew.[4] Many people have heard of Sodom and about Lot's wife and the pillar of salt. But third grade Sunday school teachers don't talk about the next part. After escaping the destruction of Sodom and settling in a cave, Lot avoided people. Lot's daughter's decided that their dad wouldn't let them hook up with any of the local guys so they decided to sleep with Lot after getting him drunk. Each got pregnant. The older daughter named her son Moab, the younger, Ben-Ammi.[5]

"It's not told how these cousins grew up. They aren't mentioned by name again until several centuries later, as

3. *Deuteronomy 23:3-6.*
4. Genesis 11:31.
5. The story is in Genesis 19:10-28.

Moses is leading the descendants of Abraham out of Egypt. The Israelites are heading to the Promised Land. As God tells Moses about the travel plans toward Canaan, he specifically warns Moses about messing with the Moabites and the Ammonites. 'I've given them their lands already,' God said. 'Because they are your relatives.'"[6]

I looked up from my note-taking. "God gave them their lands?'"

"You are going to have to read it yourself from Deuteronomy. But yes, just as God was giving Canaan to Israel, he had already given the land east of the Jordan River to these distant relatives. But the Moabites and Ammonites didn't seem to care much for their cousins. They may not have known about God's caution to Moses. They may not have understood that the land they had was at God's pleasure. First, they refused to offer any water to the Israelites. Then, they got a prophet named Balaam to curse them."

"Is that the talking donkey story?"

"Exactly. But we don't have time for that. Look it up for yourself.[7] And then, after Balaam failed, they slept with the Israelites."

"You mean made a treaty?"

"No. I mean some Moabite women seduced some Israelite men, both physically and spiritually.[8] What Balaam couldn't accomplish with curses had now been done."

"So, now we're back to what you said earlier. You were

6. Deuteronomy 2:16-23.
7. Numbers 22-24.
8. Numbers 25:1-5.

quoting Moses. And that's why you were so vehement about Tobiah, with your 'you have no share.' That was all about Tobiah's heritage."

Nehemiah nodded. "Tobiah took notice. As you already mentioned, he emerged as my most sophisticated opponent. All through the planning and attacks, Tobiah is part of the team. And then you discover that Shecaniah, one of the nobles, was Tobiah's father-in-law. And Tobiah's son married the daughter of Meshullam, one of the most prolific builders of the wall.[9]

"These alliances caused three big problems for me. First, Tobiah heard everything that was happening inside the rebuilding process. He knew exactly how well we were doing. Second, all of his friends and family kept telling me that Tobiah was a good guy, that he couldn't be like the other opponents. And third, Tobiah kept writing me threatening letters, based on all his information and relationships."[10]

"So how long did all his work against you last? You got the wall built in spite of him, right?"

Nehemiah smiled, sadly. "But have you forgotten that rebuilding the wall was just the first step? And in many ways the simplest? I was also committed to rebuilding the nation, to restoring the people to faithful living. And Tobiah was persistent, as persistent as I was. As we already have dis-

---

9. Nehemiah 6:17-19. Meshullam had built two sections, as mentioned in Nehemiah 3:4 and 3:30.
10. Nehemiah 6:17-19.

cussed, while I was gone to Susa, Tobiah talked his way into a little apartment in a temple storeroom."

"You know that he's a perfect illustration of his family's relationship with the Israelites," I said. "Saul's first battle after becoming king of Israel was responding to an attack by the Ammonite king.[11] Then David and his army fought against them for two seasons of battle after an Ammonite king made David his first battle.[12]

Nehemiah nodded. "And did you notice that David's seduction of Bathsheeba happened during the second of those campaigns? It's almost like the situation with Balaam."[13]

"I wonder," I reflected, "if David's fierceness about destroying the Ammonites contributed to Tobiah's resolve to frustrate you. David was brutal."

"I'm not sure," Nehemiah sounded thoughtful. "The shaming and brutality David demonstrated were consistent with the way conquests happened in those days. Be careful of using your standards of justice to judge peoples before you, or even people in your day.

"That said, in the centuries after this Ezekiel and Zephaniah both talk in prophecy about what will happen to the Ammonites because of their defiance of God and rejoicing over the destruction of the temple.[14] Both of those prophets

11. 1 Samuel 11:1-11.
12. 1 Chronicles 19.
13. The account in 1 Chronicles 19 merely notes that David didn't go with the army. In 2 Samuel 10-12, we read the whole story of Uriah and Bathsheeba and David right in the middle of the Ammonite battles.
14. See Ezekiel 25:1-7 and Zephaniah 2:8-11.

talk about what God will do to discipline Israel for disobedience, and that's why we had so much work to do rebuilding the wall. But God also warned the Ammonites about their mocking of Him."

We sat quietly for awhile. The story of the Ammonites is sobering. The way that it played out through Tobiah helped me understand again that Nehemiah's memoirs are a remarkable summary of the whole story of God's work with Israel.

Finally, I spoke. "I won't make you go back into the story of Tobiah again. But I want to see if I understand.

1. *Leaders need to know the full story of their opponents to guide their responses.*

2. *Resistance, especially spiritual resistance, can have deep roots.*

3. *Tribal tensions, family tensions, can last a long time.*

4. *Even after the rest of the people relax, leaders need to stay alert.*

5. *Little compromises can have big consequences.*

6. *God waits a long long time for people to change.*"

"That's pretty good," he said. "I think we're almost done with our conversations. I think you are almost ready to move on to your own great work."

I turned away. I knew he was right. But I didn't want that last conversation.

THE LAST
CONVERSATION

Nehemiah 13

"How do we finish this?" I asked Nehemiah.

He shrugged and shook his head. "That's not my problem. I completed my great work. You have to finish yours, great or not."

"But you had a hard time wrapping up your memoir, didn't you? I mean, you were pretty frustrated at the end of your story."

"Is that how you read it? I did get a little indignant when I came back and saw what had happened to the people, but I wasn't frustrated at the end."

"You're going to have to help me see that," I said. "Because you were pulling out hair."

He smiled. "It made an impression. But you need to look closely at the stories. I was making a point about promises. Let me suggest a pattern for looking at those last three stories. Look for: 1) What was wrong; 2) What I said and did; 3) What I prayed."

I took a couple minutes to read Nehemiah 13:10-14. And then I said, "Okay, in the first story the Levites weren't getting their allowance. So you said, 'Why is the house of God neglected?' And then you called the Levites back to work, you called the nobles to accountability, and you appointed responsible leaders. You prayed that God would remember you for your service."

"Good. That one was easy," he said. "But I want you to notice something. These people were doing exactly what they had promised not to do."

"What do you mean?" I said.

"Look back at the promises we all made.[1] There is great detail in our promises about bringing the appropriate tithes and offerings. We go to great lengths about all the first of every crop stuff."

"You know, I'm curious. I remember back to a question I asked you when we talked about that confession and commitment. I asked you who wrote it. And you said, if I remember, that it was the Levites. Is there so much detail about the Levites written in Chapter 10 because they wrote the vows? Was it a vested interest thing?"[2]

Nehemiah sat up very straight.

"I'm not trying to pick on anything," I said very quickly. "But I notice that in the promises, there is a lot of detail on

---

1. Recorded in Nehemiah 10:28-39.
2. I resisted the pun of calling it a vestment interest thing. Nehemiah doesn't always understand my puns.

that part, but not much detail on the Sabbath-keeping or on the marriage to the peoples around. On the other hand, in your last words here, there isn't much detail about the offerings, but you go into great detail about the other two problems. I'm just wondering."

He relaxed a little. But he didn't offer any explanation.

I went on, looking at Nehemiah 13:15-22. "Look at the detail you give about the next problem you saw. People were treading wine presses and filling bags of grain and loading them on donkeys and bringing them into Jerusalem and selling them. All of these were happening on the Sabbath. And then there were people from the coast who lived in Jerusalem and were running a fish-import business on the Sabbath."

I started laughing. "I just realized what the detail tells us. When you locked the gates and made the vendors sit outside all night and all day..." I couldn't stop laughing.

Nehemiah looked at me.

Between laughs I gasped, "The fish vendors. Loads of fish. Fresh Mediterranean fish. An extra day in the hot sun. You were so cruel."

"I wasn't cruel," he said. "I was merely keeping the Law."

"I know," I said, settling down. "I understand completely your perspective. As you reminded the leadership, one of the key reasons the people were exiled was because they did not keep the Sabbath.[3]

"But you acted with such directness. Just like you pro-

3. 2 Chronicles 36:21.

tected the builders of the walls with your own men, you had *your* people take action to close the gates; and then you trained the people who were actually responsible to take over. And come on, you have to admit that there is a bit of fun in the way you treated the vendors. 'Once or twice they spent the night outside.' If that's not playing with them, nothing is."[4]

Nehemiah finally smiled. "Sometimes you need to accomplish the task. If you wait for people to get motivated, the problem will get worse. And if the vendors ever questioned my commitment, two weeks of bringing fish and fresh vegetables and having to smell it all the way home stopped that."

"I love your prayer," I said. "You are talking about God's compassion and lovingkindness. We don't think much about God being that way in your part of the Bible."

Nehemiah shook his head. "I don't understand that angry God/nice God idea you think about sometimes. My whole life was about watching God have patience, watching God give wisdom and strength to me, a servant of the enemy king, moving me from the palace in Susa to rebuilding the wall of Jerusalem. How astonishing is that? How compassionate is that?"

"Is that what made you so upset about the mixed marriages? I mean, you were pulling out people's hair."

Nehemiah smiled sadly. "I know. It sounds awful. But

---

4. Nehemiah's leadership approach is powerful. Taking immediate action to stop the sin and then training others to handle the leadership would be worth its own lesson.

I grew up with the stories of the kings moving away from God. I remembered the marrying that happened with Moabites in the wilderness.[5] I remember the way that Solomon became the third and last of the kings of a united Israel, how the wisest man who ever lived ended up losing track of what he believed because marriage became merely political and pleasurable.

"When I lived, tribes worshipped tribal gods. (I think that's still true for you.) You protected the reputation of your God with everything. And when your God had brought you out of Egypt, had brought you out of Babylon, you made sure that everyone in your midst worshipped God. So when Rahab and Ruth came into Israel, they made a commitment to God first. They changed tribes.[6] Ruth said it clearly to Naomi: 'Your people will be my people, your God will be my God.'[7] Though both of them ended up married and part of the lineage of Messiah, marriage came after commitment.[8]

"As I was walking around Jerusalem, I kept hearing the voices speaking the languages of our adversaries. When I looked closer, I realized that it was coming from children, children born since I had been gone. And I knew what was happening. The men were marrying the women from other nations and letting them raise the children in their own lan-

5. Numbers 25.
6. Rahab's story is in Joshua 2 and 6.
7. Ruth 1:16.
8. Matthew 1:1-6.

guage, in that tribe, in that religion. For the sake of sex, our men had abandoned God. And in that moment, I lost it.

"I had no family. I had given up everything for this city, this people, for the rebuilding of the walls and the nation. So yes, I was incensed. I think I felt like one of the prophets. And if you read Malachi, he sounds much the same.[9] I attacked. I lectured. I made my point."

I nodded. "You made your point. It feels over the top to me, but I wasn't there. And the more I think about your closeness to God, to God's work, to your reading of God's word, I find it hard to be critical. I'm not sure how to apply it, but I am thinking."

Nehemiah lifted his coffee cup. "That why my story is here. To make you think. To make you wrestle with how one person lived out his great work for God."

He drank the dregs and set the mug down.

"You're not going, are you?" I asked.

"What's more to say?" he replied. "We've covered it all. The rest is for you."

"But I want to ask you about the end. The woodpile. Ever since I read that a few months back, I've wanted to talk to you about it. I have this sentimental picture of an old executive pastor, knowing that the people were going to lose track of their promises and forget to pay the fire bill, loading up extra wood on his way out of office. But that's not what happened, was it?"

---

9. Malachi was the last prophet in the Old Testament. As we said in the last chapter, some believe that he was in Jerusalem during the time that Nehemiah was back in Susa. He speaks bluntly about intermarriage in Malachi 2:11-12.

"Nope. You've been reading it more closely this time. When we made all those promises back in chapter 10, we divided up the schedule for bringing wood for the altar. And so I was just keeping our word. I made sure that the temple and the priests and the Levites and infrastructure (both of offerings for the altar and wood to fire the altar) were in place and functioning well.

"This isn't a sentimental ending to the book, as much as you would like to make it so. It's about continuing to do the work you promised to do, regardless of what other people do. That's what makes you a leader."

"And so your last words are just about continuing your work?"

"No, my last words are a prayer: 'Remember me with favor, O Lord.'"

And he was gone.

And then I cried.

Epilogue

I haven't talked with Nehemiah for awhile. I miss him. And there are so many things that I want to know about him.

I want to understand why gates mattered so much to him. They are mentioned many times. They were burned. They were barred. Why did he care?

I want to understand why Sabbath mattered so much to him. It's a theme throughout the book.

I want to understand more about the piles of wood. We talked a bit in the last chapter, but there is so much more I think.

And I want to know how he felt after spending his whole life working on a great work, only to watch everything fall apart. Because it did fall apart. Although Malachi is the last book in the Old Testament, Nehemiah's words are historically the last words. And the wall was breached again, the temple profaned and then rebuilt by Herod.

Someday we'll talk again. Face-to-face. Until then, I'll pay attention to the work in front of me. I invite you to do the same. In the meantime, I'd love to talk with you. Drop me a line at jon@anewroutine.com.

Cordially,

Jon

Bibliography

I know that there are many books about Nehemiah (the book) and
Nehemiah (the person), practical study books about leadership
and management and non-professional religious people. I know
that they exist, but I've not read any of them, nor have I written
one.

On the other hand, I have looked at several commentaries
about Nehemiah to make sure that my conversations are consistent with what is known about Nehemiah.

Brown, Raymond. *The Message of Nehemiah*. The Bible Speaks
Today Commentary. Downers Grove, IL: InterVarsity Press,
1998.

Hamilton, Victor. *Handbook on the Historical Books*. Grand Rapids,
MI: Baker Academic, 2001.

Kidner, Derek. *Ezra and Nehemiah*. Tyndale Old Testament Commentaries. Downers Grove, IL: InterVarsity Press, 2009. Origi-
nally published 1979.

Payne, J. Barton. "1,2 Chronicles" in Volume 4, The Expositor's
Bible Commentary. Regency Reference Library: Grand Rapids,
MI, 1988.

Williamson, H.G.M. *Ezra, Nehemiah*. Word Bible Commentary.
Nashville: Thomas Nelson, 1985.

THE LIST OF LESSONS

Several of the chapters have lists of lessons. Here's a collection of all the lists.

NEHEMIAH'S PASSION

Chapter 1

"If you had something that mattered that much, wouldn't you start working on it, no matter what?"

NEHEMIAH'S PRAYER

Chapter 2

1. Every day I said, 'God you are the faithful one, the committed one. Please listen to me.'
2. Every day I said, 'We have sinned. Generations of us, yes, but my family too. And I have sinned, God.' That reminder was important to me as I was learning about sharing and justice and compassion. I learned to look at my own behavior.
3. Every day I reminded God about the stories of repentance from Moses and from Isaiah. And when I did that, I was reminding myself.

4. Every day I wanted to be ready for serving the King.

NEHEMIAH'S FIVE STEPS TO AN ACTION PLAN

Chapter 4

1. A clear picture of what was wrong.
2. A simple confidence that God was involved from the start.
3. A simple proposal of what to do.
4. A specific plan of how to proceed.
5. A commitment to act on the plan.

NEHEMIAH'S FIVE LESSONS FOR BUILDING A WALL

Chapter 5

1. What looks like a line might be a circle.
2. Most of the people rebuilding the wall didn't come with me. They were on location and had been for years.
3. Everyone's story needs to be told.
4. Not everyone is going to work the same way.
5. Most people work hardest on what's closest to their heart

NEHEMIAH'S FIVE STEPS OF CONFLICT MANAGEMENT.

Chapter 6

1. In the face of verbal challenge, respond with simple truth.
2. In the face of insults, pray.
3. In the face of threats, pray and post a guard.
4. In the face of an opponent's mobilizing, implement a clear plan, which includes meaningful action, leadership strategy and reminding the people of the purpose.
5. For long-term protection, lay out a clear defense that is sustainable. It gives the people something at their back so they can go about the work.

NEHEMIAH'S SIX SIMPLE STEPS TO REMEDY JUSTIFIED WHINING

Chapter 7

1. First, take a very deep breath.
2. Second, confront the leaders who permit it.
3. Third, call everyone together and clearly outline the problem.
4. Fourth, explain what everyone can do to solve it, looking to the Bible for support.
5. Fifth, bring the leaders together for a public commitment.
6. Sixth, make the promises visual.

WHAT MAKES A GREAT WORK?

Chapter 8

1. Something about it makes you weep.
2. You have to take lots of small steps that don't seem like they will get you anywhere.
3. Doing the work transforms you.
4. God calls you to do it.
5. It matters enough that you ache when you can't accomplish it quickly enough, and it's big enough that you can't accomplish it quickly enough.
6. It is not about you.
7. It takes so long that you can't do it in a day, but the choices of each day matter in whether you can get it done.
8. You may not know anything about how to do the work.
9. You cannot not do it.

FIVE REASONS TO REPEAT THE STORIES

Chapter 11

1. As you lead, remind people of the significant problem you are solving together.
2. As you lead, remind people of God's involvement from the start.
3. As you lead, remind the people of God's power.
4. As you lead, make the lessons visual.

5. As you lead, live out the stories that God gave you to live.

The Heart of the Story

Chapter 12

The book of Nehemiah constantly tells the stories of redemption, rejection, repentance, and renewal. God redeems us. We reject God. We repent of our rejection. God renews his promises. And the cycle starts. Chapter 9 reviews it clearly so that if all someone reads is just this one book, they get the story of a man who followed God, and they get the story of a people who didn't.

Four Lessons about Lists of Names

Chapter 14

1. The **records** matter. That's why we kept them.
2. The **threads** of history matter. That's why we trace people and families and tribes through generations.
3. The **people** matter. Each name on each list is a person, created and loved by God. Like me. Like you.
4. The **people's interaction with geography** matters. Real people built the wall. Real people marched on the wall. Real people stood in front of the wall and explained what God said and Ezra read.

Six ways Nehemiah kept focus

Chapter 15

1. He tried to get his priorities from God.
2. He talked with God.
3. He kept the routines.
4. He reviewed the stories
5. He didn't get nearly as sidetracked worrying about what people were going to think.
6. He just kept going.

Four truths about leaders and promises

Chapter 16

1. Make sure that when you make promises, you make them about the things that matter. At least that way, when people wander, they are wandering from what is important, and when you call them to repentance, it's a call that is a call back to God.
2. When you are a leader, remind people of the promises that they made. Our job is to keep people focused on what we all committed to. It's why we have been called by people and by God. More than anything else we do, calling people to faithfulness matters.
3. When you are a servant, you have to follow God, no matter what.
4. People struggle to obey. That's how it is.

A SUMMARY OF LESSONS FROM TOBIAH

Chapter 18

1. Leaders need to know the full story of their opponents to guide their responses.
2. Resistance, especially spiritual resistance, can have deep roots.
3. Tribal tensions, family tensions, can last a long time.
4. Even after the rest of the people relax, leaders need to stay alert.
5. Little compromises can have big consequences.
6. God waits a long long time for people to change.

ACKNOWLEDGEMENTS

I wish I knew why I started reading *Nehemiah* during the summer of 2012. I don't. What I do know is that Tony Covely sat in my office and said that he'd love for the guys in our church to "do something." And I said, "I could teach the book of Nehemiah in Sunday school."

As a result of that conversation, I taught the first passes through this material in a Wednesday evening Bible study and in a Sunday morning study. And a college-age class went through this with me. Thanks to my Grabill Missionary church family for their patience and questions and to our small group for keeping us busy every Saturday night.

I wanted to write more reflectively and so started a weekly email. In the first of those emails, I found myself talking with Nehemiah. I am grateful that he decided to sit in my office, and that a group of people read those emails every week. Some of those readers, particularly Becky McCray and Rob Hatch, have been more helpful on this project than they know.

Hope Swanson and I have had many conversations in the car while I drove her places. One of those led to the decision to turn my writings into a book. And led Hope to talking a prof into letting her edit an early version of this manuscript for an independent study. Then, when I wasn't sure whether to keep working, she wrote the email that turned into the Foreword.

Nancy Swanson, with whom I have been married since 1983, read the weekly emails, endured conversations, encouraged me to write, kept the television turned down, and prayed. She's read A Great Work twice, looking for mistakes and finding value. And she's the one who said, "What's the project this will fund?" Together we'll be using the profits to encourage Nehemiah-shaped projects that rebuild walls and people.

This book is dedicated to Arnold C. Swanson who loved Nehemiah. Dad often said, "the only thing you can make a man out of is a boy" and so he devoted his working life to that purpose. It was a Nehemiah-shaped project, and he was faithful to the end.

And I don't know why God let me have these conversations with Nehemiah, but I am grateful beyond words. I miss them already.

ABOUT THE AUTHOR

Jon Swanson is passionate about helping people emotionally understand God's work.

He is a husband, father, and associate pastor living in Fort Wayne, Indiana. He has worked in higher education in Texas and Indiana. He and Nancy have been married more than thirty years and have two children, Andrew (married with Allie) and Hope. Jon is ordained by the Missionary Church and has a PhD in communication studies (UT-Austin). He writes regularly at http://300wordsaday.com.

Since 2000, Jon has worked as an associate pastor at two churches. He has produced videos, talked with people needing financial help, married and buried people, and helped other people understand how to accomplish their work.

Since 1995, he has taught in many settings. He taught communication and management courses for college credit. He has taught many Sunday school classes and small groups and preached. Rather than teaching from study guides, he walks people through books of the Bible, including extensive studies of Malachi, Nehemiah, Philippians, Psalms, Colossians, the Sermon on the Mount, and 1 John. During the past two years, he has taught an online course for pastors studying church administration and is developing two more.

Jon is the author of three ebooks: *Lent for non-Lent People*, *Learning a New Routine*, and *Anticipation: an Advent Reader*.

Made in the USA
Charleston, SC
31 May 2016